MARJORIE SYKES
QUAKER – GANDHIAN

D1549787

Cover illustration: Original painting of Marjorie Sykes by Edith Cooper

Marjorie at Santiniketan

Marjorie Sykes
Quaker - Gandhian

by

Martha Dart

Sessions Book Trust
in association with Woodbrooke College

ISBN 1 85072 125 4

A companion edition for Indian distribution is being
published by The Academy of Gandhian Studies,
Hyderabad 500 044, India. For USA, copies may be obtained
from Pendle Hill Bookstore, Wallingford, Pa 19086, USA.

Printed on paper obtained from trees grown in maintained forests

Printed in 11 on 12 pt Plantin Typeface
by William Sessions Limited
The Ebor Press, York, England

Contents

Illustrations

Foreword

MARJORIE SYKES has the rare quality of manifesting in her life and thought her inmost convictions. These I believe to have risen in her from sources that, although widely separated from each other in time, circumstance and inspiration, were strangely alike in their essentials, namely the Quaker and the Gandhian.

She came to know both at first hand in her long Indian encounter that began more than six decades ago. If Marjorie would appear to some as a Quaker Gandhian, she would appear to others as a Gandhian Quaker. If her Indian friends learned to love and respect Quaker insights through the way she lived them out, her Western friends perceived the essence of Gandhian philosophy in the way she sought to practice it. Whether as a Quaker drawn into the Gandhian spell, or as a Gandhian rooted in Quakerism, Marjorie is the last surviving example of the fusion of the two in one person.

Nor was this all: association with Marjorie has been a continuing lesson in the practical art of living without things that one can sensibly do without, and indeed ought to do without in the best Quaker-Gandhian tradition. I never ceased to be amazed at how she could live so richly in body and mind with so little of material possessions around her. Whilst she lived in Rasulia, my greatest joy in visiting there was the anticipation of being looked after by her so remarkably well despite the down-to-earth basicness in everything and the apparent scarcity of the goods and services that one might ordinarily have regarded as indispensable for reasonable well-being.

There were also editorial lessons in abundance for me to learn from her. Marjorie's gift for condensing a whole page into a paragraph, a paragraph into a sentence, without losing one bit that mattered, came from that sharpness of mind that enabled her to grasp the essence of things quickly. In writing and speaking, as in life, she would exercise her faculty to sift the substantial from the trivial. Although not trained as a historian, she had the historian's instinct for facts, and more than the historian's passion for saying only what has been verified. Nothing annoyed her more in what others said or wrote than unverified statements or assumptions.

Above all, it has been wonderful simply to know Marjorie as a person, and to come to see in the process that for all the seeming severity of her aspect she had an engaging sense of humour and the capacity to laugh and to relax, and to enjoy her numerous friend-ships with people of varied backgrounds and circumstances. It has been impossible to escape being influenced in some way by such a person.

P. T. Thomas, Co-Editor, *The Friendly Way*, June 1990

Preface

MARJORIE SYKES has been a good friend since we first met in India in 1967. She has lived through and been part of a remarkable era in Indian history which is fast passing and there are fewer and fewer people still living who have had this experience. Many people, I included, have tried to persuade Marjorie to write her life story but she has had other priorities. I am grateful that she has agreed to have me write her biography.

Marjorie herself has been a continuing help, reading the text and making useful additions and corrections. I am especially grateful to her for the chapter on her childhood for which she is my main source and much of which she has written herself. I am also grateful to Marjorie's sister, Kathleen Sykes, and her niece, Dorothy Bayes, for childhood and family pictures.

I feel special gratitude to my husband, Leonard Dart, for his constant support, wisdom and practical help, including putting all the text on the word-processor countless times and in doing the needful with photographs and maps. The book could not have been done without him.

I have enjoyed writing this book while at Woodbrooke College, Quaker Study Centre, with which Marjorie has had many associations too. To have been living this year in the room in which Gandhi stayed for a brief visit to Woodbrooke in 1931 has been an added special joy to me. Chris Lawson, Senior Tutor, has been a constant inspiration, editor, and advisor and a practical help in every way. I want to express appreciation to Christina Lawson, the Librarian, for her patience and kindness in helping me find references, and to Janey O'Shea, Quaker Studies Tutor, for her thoughtful reading of the text and her helpful suggestions, and to all the Woodbrooke staff who in various ways have made things easier.

This may be the place to tell American readers that in deference to Marjorie and all British friends involved, I have tried to use British spelling and grammar. Peter Hardy, Barbara Bowman and Phyllis Topping have patiently edited the manuscript for 'Americanisms', and lapses in British spelling and punctuation, as well as making helpful suggestions. Ram and Stephanie Ramamurthy have been a great help and support as has the staff of the Friends House Library in London.

It would be impossible to mention all the people who have been of help in the production of this book. I am especially grateful to all those who responded to my request for memories and impressions of Marjorie. Many of them are mentioned in the text along with their quotes and I am very grateful to them and to others not mentioned. It has been especially helpful to have memories of Marjorie's early years in India from Florence Theophilus and Rani Dawson (neé Simon) who knew her, both when they were children at Bentinck School, and as colleagues later at Women's Christian College.

I am grateful to P. T. Thomas of Bangalore for his Foreword and the loan of his letters from Marjorie. 'Tom' as he likes to be known to his friends, has a Ph.D in Sociology from Manchester University and is retired from being Principal of the School of Social Work in Indore. Letters sent by Brenda Fraser and Georgeana Foster have been particularly helpful, as have the photographs sent by Martin Ludlam, Agnes and Peter Stein and Marius Boelsma. I want to thank Margaret Glover for letting me use reproductions of both her drawing and her portrait of Marjorie. Edith Cooper, a close personal friend of both Marjorie's and mine, has been pleased that I wanted to use the sensitive portrait which she made of Marjorie in 1976 on the cover. She is aware of my gratitude.

In the last 30 years there has been a considerable change in the meaning of certain words. Upper high school and college age students who in an earlier generation were referred to as 'girls' are now called 'young women', and this has been done except in quotes. The same is true of the term 'negro' in the United States. In the early 60's the term was just changing from 'negro' to 'black', and the quotes in the chapter on North America reflect this.

The reader will find under *Sources*, the wide range of sources to which I am indebted and I take the opportunity here to express my appreciation for all of them. I hope I have traced any copyright material but apologise to authors if not.

Martha Dart, April 1993

Prologue

'BECAUSE OF MARJORIE SYKES, I know I, as a woman, can be strong in myself. I can, if I choose to, do what I feel to be important even if it is not quite as most people would do. That is a very precious gift which I received as a child from Marjorie even if she was unaware of it.'

'It is not easy to sum up such a person as Marjorie Sykes. She gave off feelings of strength that come what may, you would be strong in her presence.'

'Marjorie's greatest contribution is her personal impact on those around her – what she is, the way she lives her life and the transforming power of her spirit.'

Where did this strength and transforming power come from?

CHAPTER ONE

Childhood and Youth 1905-23

MARJORIE'S ROOTS are in a Yorkshire family in the Pennine Hills in the Huddersfield area, specifically a village called Linthwaite. Sykes is the occupational name for the cottage weavers who lived by the 'Syke', the moorland stream in whose waters the fleece were scoured to provide the clean wool for their work. Later Sykes generations moved to the woollen mills of Huddersfield in Western Yorkshire, where Marjorie's uncles and cousins worked. Her father, Wilfrid Sykes, however, decided to enter a teacher's training college and was chosen to go on for additional training in science at Dresden in Germany.

On his return to England he was appointed Headmaster of a school serving a very poor coal-mining village at Mexborough in South Yorkshire. On this modest but assured salary he married a fellow teacher from Huddersfield, Amelia (Millie) Maxon, and they settled into the home provided for the Headmaster adjoining the school. They had both been brought up in comparative poverty, but also in thrift, cleanliness, and piety and the conditions in which the mining families lived were a shock and a challenge.

Marjorie was born in that school house on the 11th May in 1905, the eldest of three children – her sister, Kathleen, two years younger and her brother, Ronald, six years younger. Marjorie remembers only little picture memories of the early years.

> One is of myself toddling around the 'scullery' in the midst of Monday morning wash day – and sitting down in a bucket of dirty water. The result was a day spent in bed while my clothes were washed and dried. Another picture is of myself hopefully planting a date seed in the dust in a corner of the asphalt yard which was our only playing space. Naturally it didn't grow!'

Marjorie and Kathleen, ages five and three (1910)

Marjorie learned to read very early, for there were plenty of children's books in the house. Publishers used to send specimen copies to Headmasters hoping for orders. Marjorie's mother remembered her at about age four, sitting on a stool reading to her little sister out of a story book, dramatising as she went along. She would be the Sea-captain in a white boat sailing across the channel to get a princess to marry a prince. The boat sank and she shouted 'Take out the baggage and let her sink!' Apparently there was some factual basis to this tale but she embellished it to the joy and thrill of her little sister.

Marjorie continued this dramatic storytelling throughout her childhood, telling bed-time stories which she made up, partly from fact, to her little sister and brother. 'Tell us the mischief stories', they would beg and she would embark on all the mischief done that day by the naughty little boys in her class in school, adding dramatic tales from her own imagination.

She loved to 'get people acting'. Later when she and Kathleen and Ronald got together with their cousins in Huddersfield, there was sure to be some kind of play. Marjorie was the oldest and consequently the stage manager and 'boss'. On the outskirts of Huddersfield was a high hill – Castle Hill – with the ruins of an old castle on top and what was once a moat around it. By that time it held no water and that was where they held their rehearsals. There were witches stirring their brew as they muttered 'Bubble – bubble – toil and trouble', and ghosts from Macbeth. The three little boys were the ghosts and when 'ghost after ghost' were to appear, the three would make a continuous procession by disappearing behind a sheet hung up as a curtain and coming out front again. Parents and aunts and uncles made up an appreciative audience. Marjorie's enthusiasm for drama has continued throughout her life and enriched her own life and the lives of her students and colleagues wherever she might be.

But that was later. When Marjorie first went to school, her father took her with him and left her in the 'infant class'.

> But [recalls Marjorie], I soon began to catch both the common children's ailments and the ever-present vermin. I had my hair clipped short, like a boy, so that it was easier to keep clean. My mother must have worried about the risk of infection both for my younger sister and for the baby brother just born. She may also have suspected – what was the fact – that I was learning in the wrong way, from playground sniggers, such matters as 'where babies came from'. I felt uneasy and said nothing; neither did she. But soon after my sixth birthday I was sent off to the junior section of the Mexborough Secondary School.

When Marjorie was a baby, her parents had her baptised, but except for that there was no public religious observance in the family, and none of the children ever went to Sunday School. Her mother did teach them the Lord's Prayer, and got them to kneel by their beds and repeat it before sleep. That was all, but as Marjorie comments, 'We might have done worse'.

Soon after she began going to the secondary school her father was transferred to another elementary school, still in Mexborough but in a cleaner part. No 'school house' was provided there, and their new home was at the end of a cul-de-sac of about a dozen little houses. They had a big wild garden, with fruit trees and bushes, on a kind of promontory surrounded on three sides by a disused stone quarry – a wonderful place for imaginative play.

The pre-adolescence years of girlhood were centred on that home and the school. Marjorie recalls:

> Kathleen and I made our first friends among the neighbours' children who came to play in our garden, climb the trees, and build 'houses' of interwoven twigs and slender branches. (One of these little friends was later to become my brother's wife.) Outside our kitchen door was a well with a hand pump, whose water was safer and more reliable than the public supply in the kitchen tap. Nearby was a little pear shaped enclosure whose dry stone walls were topped with earth – a ready-made garden house which we called 'the Grotto' and where we played at house-keeping and 'cooked' cakes compounded of chickweed and mud. (Looking back now, I guess that this 'Grotto' was the original builder's way of using the material extracted when the well was dug.)

> My father [continues Marjorie], rejoiced in the garden and spent long evening hours there. He gave us each a tiny plot where we could do as we liked, and where I sowed seeds with more hope of success than with the date stone in the dust. At school also we little ones were given similar plots, and as I learned and grew older I began to help with the 'proper' garden. On Sunday mornings there were long walks with father through the fields and woods, where we two sisters were introduced to the wonders of wild nature, while mother enjoyed comparative peace with only my toddler brother left at home!

Marjorie remembers how she stood at her father's side as he bent over his garden seeds and said, 'Isn't it marvellous? So tiny

and they look so much alike. But how differently they will grow.'
He never categorised people or thought of nations, sects or class
as stereotypes. He also taught Marjorie what she was to know later
in India as *Nishkama Karma* 'to carry out one's duty uninfluenced
by personal desire'. This her father *lived* in his long hours of labour
for the welfare of the children in his school. As he lay dying in the
Spring of 1940, he said to his cousin and closest friend, 'There's
only one thing that matters – learning to be unselfish'.

> Inside the house, my mother was always *there*. We hung
> around the kitchen, industriously scraping up and eating the
> tasty remains which adhered to the mixing bowl after the cakes
> had been put in the oven. Mother gave us bits of pastry to
> shape as we pleased and put to cook alongside the 'proper'
> pies. At school there were practical cookery classes where I
> made a small loaf of bread, or a jam tart, and proudly brought
> it home.

When Marjorie was a little older and stronger she could help knead
the dough at home – seven pounds at a time. She and Kathleen
helped their mother make 'Parkin', a special Yorkshire cake made
with oatmeal, sour milk, eggs, treacle and ginger, poured into a
square pan lined with buttered paper. This was put into the oven
at the end of the baking when the temperature was lower. It made
a fairly moist, chewy cake, differing from gingerbread because
oatmeal was used instead of flour. After a light supper (called High
Tea in Yorkshire) of scrambled eggs or something similar, there
would be a piece of Parkin and a glass of milk before going to bed.

Marjorie and her sister, Kathleen, learned to sew early on. Their
mother cut out the frocks to the right size and they did the stitching by hand in small neat stitches – a habit which Marjorie has
carried on throughout her life no matter where she happened to be.

Marjorie was nine years old when war was declared in August
1914 and she has never forgotten the heavy sense of disaster that
hung in the air. She remembers:

> War held no glamour or glory for me. A beloved teacher disap-
> peared from our school; she was German and had become an
> 'enemy alien' overnight. We heard talk of the cruel harassment
> she had suffered from the 'patriotic' hooligans of the town. We
> children were bewildered, our parents were grieved and angry.

5

Her father had close friends in Germany from the year he had spent studying in Dresden. Photographs of them hung in the living room of their home and he would often speak of them with affection and wonder how they were and how the war affected them.

In 1916 things changed as the war dragged on and military conscription was introduced in Britain. Her father, who was near the upper age limit and Headmaster of a school, could probably have been exempt. Although he had no illusions about war and knew it to be evil, he struggled with himself to see where his duty lay and finally decided he should join the army. He signed up as a private soldier and was sent for the regular preliminary training in England. When set to clean windows, he aroused comment by insisting on cleaning *both* sides – that was the standard of his Yorkshire home!

It was not long, however, before the authorities realised that this private soldier was a teacher with scientific knowledge; they gave him the rank of sergeant and set him to train the officer recruits in the science of gunnery. Finally he was himself given an officer's commission and sent to the fighting lines in command of an artillery unit.

Marjorie recalls:

It was then that Mother's anxiety really began. After the birth of my brother she had never been really strong, and during my girlhood a woman would come over once or twice a week and help with the heavier household work. She was a desperately poor widow woman who lived in a one-room house behind the shopping street, but for us all she was a member of the family to be honoured and respected. But she could not lighten mother's burden of fear for her husband's safety on the battlefield, nor for her three school-age children when night air-raids began, aimed at the great Sheffield Steel Works a few miles away. When at last in November, 1918, the fighting ceased, it was followed by another anxiety – the influenza epidemic which, having devastated India, spread through Europe also. I was the one who caught the infection; I have no memory of my father's coming home, for when he did so, I was delirious and unconscious. My parents' devoted care pulled me through.

Although Marjorie's father was home again, the two years of military service, so different from his normal work, had left him restless; he felt unable to settle at once into teaching. A cousin who was also a close friend and whom the children called 'uncle', invited him to help in a little mill he was running in the village of Horbury just outside Wakefield. He was making rugs with clippings of warm felt to cover the cold stone floors of Yorkshire kitchens. Marjorie's father decided to do so, and the family left Mexborough and rented a house in Horbury. By that time Marjorie had pretty well recovered, though the doctor advised that she should stay out of school until the Autumn. But the move that Spring completely exhausted her mother; and they had no sooner reached Horbury than she became seriously ill.

> For the next five months [recalls Marjorie], I took charge of the household, cooked and scrubbed, washed the family's clothes, and mended them, got the younger ones off to school, nursed Mother, and in the odd moments tackled the neglected garden – a wonderful experience of 'learning through work'.
>
> I well remember the day when, as I was working in my mother's room, she suddenly smiled at me and said, 'You know, when you were born, I was a bit disappointed that my first child wasn't a boy. Now I'm *glad* you are a girl'. I was silent – too moved to speak – but I swelled inwardly with pride and happiness; I who had so often secretly wished I *was* a boy, suddenly saw (although I could not have expressed it) how much satisfaction there might be in being a girl. From that moment I was content with my womanhood.

Years later when she was in her seventies and a Friend-in-Residence at Pendle Hill, a Quaker study centre near Philadelphia in the United States, she was described as 'such a well-organised, effective woman – and so *womanly* – tender and caring under that determined capability she has'.

By the Autumn her mother had regained her strength and Marjorie joined a new school, the Wakefield High School for Girls. Classes for an adolescent were interesting and challenging. Marjorie remembers the thrill of being introduced to Milton's *Paradise Lost* by an enthusiastic teacher. The religious education of the school made a strong impression. Morning assemblies always

School Crest and Motto
Wakefield High School for Girls

Hear the ancients watchword ringing
   'Each for all and all for God'.
May it nerve and brace our spirits
   As we march along life's road.

Each for all, the school's great motto
   May we never from it swerve.
All for God, O help us Father
   Whose we are and Whom we serve.

Each for all, O Father make us
   Strong to serve and to endure.
All for God, so shall our service
   Single hearted be and pure.

Step by step direct Thy children
   Until all the way be trod,
Living, loving, learning, labouring
   Each for all and all for God.

ended with the quiet singing of the Biblical prayer: 'Lead me, Lord. Lead me in Thy righteousness. Make Thy way plain before my face.' In her senior class, the Headmistress would read a great variety of thought-provoking writings, and encourage the students to think matters out for themselves. Then there was the school motto, 'Each for All and All for God', and the school hymn based on it. More than 70 years later Marjorie could still sing that hymn to herself with gratitude.

Meanwhile her father's love for teaching had reasserted itself, and he was appointed to a village school just outside Wakefield. When Marjorie was about to enter her final school year, however, he was transferred to Conisborough, a coal mining community adjacent to Mexborough, to the kind of school with which he had struggled in his first working years. By that time Marjorie was working for entrance to Cambridge, and it would not have been wise to change schools at that stage. In Wakefield, the High School maintained a small boarding house for those who needed it, and that was the solution.

Those who lived in the boarding house attended the beautiful Cathedral Church at Wakefield:

> There [remembered Marjorie], I absorbed the lovely music of the ritual, and the magnificent prose cadences of the Book of Common Prayer. I still have my father's copy of that Prayer Book, dating back to his own college days, and given to me, with no word spoken, at the time when I could use it. In school some of the great passages of English poetry 'haunted me like a passion' in much the same way as did the prayers. There was no division between the 'sacred' and the 'secular'. I was being prepared to understand to some extent how other great religious poetry, such as the *Qur'an* or the *Vedas*, may have a 'meaning beyond meaning' for those whose roots are in the Islamic or Hindu culture.

That last year at school brought other excitements. Marjorie recalls:

> Travelling south for the first time for the Cambridge entrance examination, I passed through Ely and visited the ancient and magnificent cathedral – an experience in a class of its own, never to be surpassed. Back at school, with the examination successfully behind me, there was leisure and zest to sample Greek; my teacher started me on Plato's story of Socrates, an inspiring narrative in beautiful simple prose. There could have been no better introduction to a lovely language.

9

I don't remember much about the classes in my Mexborough school. But I do remember with gratitude one thing that in my mind didn't count as classes – the periodic excursions led by our history teacher. She would take us to interesting places, all within easy reach. There were old village churches, one with a 'leper squint', another with a stone cross carved in ancient runic characters. There was a ruined monastery; best of all there was the great Norman Keep of Consiborough Castle, the setting of Walter Scott's *Ivanhoe*. In the hands of that teacher history became human and alive, and in Wakefield it continued to be human and alive. It was exciting to find the Christmas shepherds in the old Wakefield 'mystery' plays feeding their sheep in 'Horbury Shroggs'!

Those years of adolescence held other interests. The country walks of Marjorie's childhood led on to a love for tramping the wide Pennine uplands; she and her sister and brother spent many happy Saturdays roaming the hills with their cousins and friends. Their parents let them go, knowing that they could read a map and use a compass, and that they had each other's company and the few pence needed for the fare home. What did it matter that there was no money for conventional holidays? This was better!

The organised games at school played a less important part in Marjorie's life, but she recalls one memorable exception:

At Wakefield we played the Canadian game, lacrosse, which being a good runner I greatly enjoyed. At that time very few English schools played it, so we had little chance of testing our skill. One Saturday, however, two county teams had arranged to play one another on our field. The weather was doubtful; Cheshire turned up, their opponents didn't. So we school girls offered to give our guests a game. By half time it was clear that we were hopelessly out-classed, so for the second half we mixed our players and had a good friendly game with two evenly-matched teams. It was a happy memory to carry away from happy school days.

CHAPTER TWO

Cambridge 1923-27

IN THE AUTUMN OF 1923, Marjorie entered Newnham College Cambridge with a college scholarship for the study of English. The course for the English Tripos (Honours degree) was a natural continuation of the intellectual interests which had been fostered in school. It combined a study of the great creative writers with an equally fascinating study of the historical and social context of their work. Intertwined with the living human history was the tracing of all the linguistic contributions – from Celtic Britain, Scandinavia and France – which have enriched the English language.

She had soon, like all her classmates, acquired a second-hand bicycle, and was attending her chosen classes, term by term, in the various college lecture rooms. Linguistic classes were held in her own college, of which the professor was a member. On the first day she listened absorbed as each student in turn repeated a simple sentence and was then told precisely and accurately in which part of the British Isles he or she had been reared!

All this was possible for a poor schoolmaster's daughter because in the early 1920's there was generous public provision for academically promising students. Grants from the West Riding of Yorkshire and the State supplemented the college scholarship so that all fees were covered and there was a little left over for personal expenses. With care, Marjorie could manage. Her father showed her how to open and operate her own bank account; that made her feel really grown up!

Wakefield High School had given her a good preparation for independent university study. The Sixth Form, the pre-university class, had a much less rigid timetable of actual teaching, with time to learn how to use a library and to work on their own. At Cambridge there was the experience and discipline of 'sound learning', the Newnham College library whose scholarly librarian became in later years a valued friend, and in later years explorations in the University Library for things Newnham could not provide. There was the fun of trying out subjects outside her chosen field, such as Dr McTaggart's open lectures in philosophy, and in listening to public debates between brilliant thinkers who had entirely different points of view. Each student had a 'tutor' in the college who directed her studies; Marjorie was soon trying to persuade hers to allow her to attend stimulating and unusual courses instead of the basic routine. 'I can read that up for myself', she would say. The argument usually ended in some form of compromise!

Cambridge had much to offer in addition to the academic. College and university societies of all kinds sought the allegiance of each new generation of newcomers, and the energies of youth found time and space for a great range of interests. Marjorie played 'fives' (hand ball), as she had done at Wakefield; the only other women's college did not, and it was fun to be able to beat some of the male college teams, as she and her partners sometimes did. Then there was the river, where she learned to manage boats – sculling in the winter, punting and canoeing in the summer, in company with friends, and sometimes, too, alone. There were summer afternoons when examinations loomed ahead, and Marjorie would take a canoe, paddle it far upstream into the quiet of the countryside, moor it in a hidden corner, and read happily amid the hum of insects and the gentle rippling of the water. Coming back to Cambridge after years in India, she found that she still knew how to handle a punt; once later at the Women's Christian College in Madras, she and a colleague who was a member of the Boat Club, took one of their Indian friends for a picnic on the Adyar River in a punt. The colleague was an Oxford graduate, and the Indian passenger sat and chuckled while Oxford and Cambridge argued vigorously about which was the right end of the punt from which to pole it!

Newnham College had four halls of residence; and a few 'out-students', whose homes were in Cambridge, were attached to each. Marjorie made friends quickly and naturally among those in her own hall, including Jean Oman, who was an out-student – her father

12

being Principal of one of the men's colleges. She also, however, made friends with an out-student from another hall, Myrtle Wright, whose father was a Cambridge doctor. Possibly this was through her former Indian classmate in Mexborough, who had come up to Newnham to read medicine at the same time as she did. They introduced her to a flourishing university society known as 'international teas', whose meetings were often held in Myrtle's home in King's Parade. Students from all over the world filled the big drawing room; there were many from India, including two or three women from Madras who were to make Marjorie welcome there a few years later. A number of the Indians had been active in Mahatma Gandhi's first 'non-cooperation movement' two years earlier, and the name 'Gandhi' became familiar to Marjorie for the first time.

In later years, given Marjorie's flair for the dramatic, she especially enjoyed taking part in parodies on Gilbert and Sullivan plays. One that she particularly remembers was a delightful topical play written by Camilla V. Wedgewood who was later a respected historian of the 17th century and considered the authority on Berlin.

Cambridge also stimulated and developed Marjorie's concern for peace. She had never forgotten a scene in her own home, soon after the family moved to Horbury. Her father sat reading the newspaper, which told of the humiliating 'peace terms' forced upon Germany by the Treaty of Versailles. 'If they go on like this', he burst out, 'there will be another war by the time Ronald is old enough to fight!' The prophesy came true; in 1939 Marjorie's brother, Ronald, a young married man with a baby, enlisted in the Royal Air Force. 'There are plenty of people we can train as pilots,' he was told, 'You are a scientist, *your* place is in the research station!' But in 1923 that was far in the future.

At Cambridge Marjorie came under the influence of teachers whose convictions about peace and social justice had been inspired directly by the life and teachings of Jesus. She began studying the Bible systematically for the fist time and it is clear from its influence on her that she had not lost anything by coming to it comparatively late.

Cambridge [wrote Marjorie], led me to see that the way of Jesus was a way of 'non-violence' – a way to be followed in the details of daily living. Jesus, not Gandhiji, was my teacher of truth and non-violence; although what I learned in Cambridge was confirmed and much enriched by what I learned later from Gandhiji and others in India.

War between nations, said Canon Charles Raven, was a denial of all that Jesus stood for. Raven was still a very young Dean when Marjorie went up to Cambridge and he 'spoke to the condition' of many students, including herself. He was in spirit very close to Friends, although Marjorie at that time was completely unaware of Friends and what they stood for. 'If there is real keenness and a

The picture of Marjorie Sykes used on her application for work in India

real group mind,' he wrote in his *Autobiography*, 'preaching can rise to the level of the purest corporate worship. Preacher and congregation together are aware of God, and of one another as in Him, and what is said is an expression of that of which all are aware, that to which all are aspiring. There are times of this kind when "the place is shaken"'. 'What about that for ideal Quaker ministry?' asked Marjorie when she read the words in later years.

Another 'Quakerly' influence was that of Edward S. Woods, then the vicar of Cambridge Church. His book *Every Day Religion* put forward the thesis that a disciple of Christ must express the love of God and neighbour in ordinary daily living. He described his vision of a truly humane society where *all* necessary work should be equally honoured and rewarded, where the skill of the coal miner in his dirty and sometimes dangerous work should be held in even higher regard than the skill of the doctor or the research scientist. As for the necessary work which is largely unskilled drudgery, like keeping the surroundings clean and healthy, why should not everyone do their share?

This for Marjorie was a new social vision, a real 'eye-opener'. It would be confirmed later by the teaching of Mahatma Gandhi in India, but at the time it was linked with two other events of her time at Cambridge. There was a conference of Christian thinkers on Politics, Economics and Citizenship, and in the Spring of 1926 there was the British General Strike which was sparked off by the widespread sense of injustice felt by manual labourers and artisans, especially the coal miners.

At Newnham, students from very different social backgrounds mixed freely; people were accepted for what they were in themselves. Friendship was a very special part of those years. Among Marjorie's close friends, along with Jean Oman and Myrtle Wright, were Ellen Cumber who read mathematics and Winifred Francis who read modern languages. Not one of them was a Quaker while at college. Myrtle joined Friends not long afterwards and devoted herself to Quaker service. Winifred and her husband Claude Wilcox also joined. Ellen and Jean Oman (later McConnell) both worked closely with Friends in tasks of reconciliation both local and international. There were many others among Marjorie's seniors and contemporaries with whom she was to work in increasing intimacy later.

15

When Marjorie herself became a senior, informal study groups met in her room. Some of the students had found a book which discussed the ways in which the less sensitive of Christian missionaries had alienated the people of other parts of the world by their negative attitude to the local culture and values and ways of life. One of the main leaders of the group was a Swedish-American student, a bit older than the others. Her father's work had taken the family to a number of countries, and she knew China well, and had experienced some of the problems described in the book. Marjorie became aware that the message of Jesus must be given with respect for the various cultural traditions of the world and a readiness to learn from them.

Marjorie spent a good deal of time during her final year at Newnham working on the 'thesis' which might be submitted, by those who wished, as an optional addition to the regular Tripos papers. She chose as her subject, William Blake, whose writings both captivated and puzzled her. When it was time for final examinations, she became ill at the very time she was to take the paper on Shakespeare, her favourite subject. Fortunately she had written the extra report. She nevertheless felt insecure about the outcome and when friends who lived in Cambridge saw her off for the Summer and said they'd let her know when the results were posted, she said, 'Oh, don't bother – unless', she said diffidently, 'it's a first place'. To her surprised delight, a telegram arrived a few days later – with the words 'First Class'! After receiving her degree at Newnham in the Summer of 1926, English Tripos (Honours BA), Cambridge Class I, she was to spend one more year at Cambridge doing teacher training.

During all these Cambridge years, college vacations were being spent at Mexborough, for her father was teaching in the nearby Conisborough school, bringing to the children 'the zest of discovery and the joy of achievement, of clean fun and adventure, of the world of beauty and imagination, of human understanding and compassion'. Marjorie describes the long evenings when she tried to help him in the preparation of his material:

> He would set to work to design and try out all kinds of practical working models, simple enough for the children themselves to make and operate, which would give them a real understanding of the common machinery of daily life. He

would also choose poems in great variety, those which would appeal to the children's sense of humour or beauty or mystery, cyclostyle them all and gather them into home-made booklets. Best of all, perhaps, he would ponder over some great incident of history and re-tell it in such a way as to awaken a child's human sympathies and bring home the lasting relevance and meaning of the story. There was excitement in all this, but also drudgery – or so it would have seemed to many people. We did not call it drudgery; we joined eagerly in the stitching of the homemade cyclostyled children's books, and also in the hours of preparation when fascinating and unusual games were made ready for occasional school parties.

Lucky children, Marjorie thought, to be in her father's school!

These experiences confirmed Marjorie's growing desire to be a teacher herself, and when she had completed her Tripos she returned to Cambridge to work for the Cambridge Teachers Diploma at the training school for teachers. It was a happy year, with new friendships, renewed joy in music, and renewed involvement in drama and the acting of plays, both for sheer enjoyment and for their educational value.

Meanwhile her interest in teaching had acquired a new dimension. During her later years at Newnham, Cambridge had been visited by young articulate teachers from universities and schools in many parts of the world, who invited Cambridge men and women to be partners with them in the education of their own people. They spoke of the urgent need that the people of the emerging nations of Africa and the East should learn to discriminate among the powerful influences from the West, so that their own cultures should not be destroyed, but enriched by the contact. Some of Marjorie's fellow students at Newnham accepted university posts in western Africa in response to this invitation; one of her close friends at the training college was off to central Africa as soon as her course was completed. Marjorie put her name down to be kept informed of any such post for which she might be qualified.

No such post was immediately in view, and she was advised to get more experience in England first. That was sensible advise; she took a junior teaching post in a school on Merseyside, on the outskirts of Liverpool, and shared a little flat with another Newnham student, one year her senior, who was teaching mathematics in the same school. The senior English mistress was a wise and helpful guide; Marjorie enjoyed setting 11-year-olds to dramatise 'Sir Roger de Coverley' and helping to produce a school play. The months went by. One Saturday in May 1928, she got word that there was an urgent request for someone to teach in South India. 'You are the only one on our list with the right qualifications', said the writer. Marjorie got on the next train for London to find out about it. There she found a young woman who, for family reasons, had just returned from teaching in the Bentinck School for Girls in Madras – a school being run by the London Missionary Society. She had photographs to show and a lot of first hand information to hand on. It appealed to Marjorie; she applied, was appointed, and prepared to leave in the Autumn for India.

Marjorie with her Father – about 1936

CHAPTER THREE

Bentinck School in Madras 1928-39

IN OCTOBER Marjorie set sail for India from Liverpool, down the Irish Sea, round France and Spain through the Bay of Biscay and through the Mediterranean Sea. For Marjorie, whose range of travel had scarcely gone beyond Yorkshire and Cambridge, each day was a new adventure. They stopped at Naples for a whole day and were able to see Mt Vesuvius and other points of interest. On then to Aden, Colombo, and round Sri Lanka to Madras, arriving in early November after a little less than four weeks at sea.

Arrival in India was exciting. When the ship had anchored in the harbour, suddenly there came on board Alice Varley, Principal of Bentinck School, and little Jagannathan, the small grandson of the man who was to teach her Tamil. Alice greeted her warmly while Jagannathan jumped up and down excitedly, saying over and over in Tamil, 'Isn't a ship wonderful? Isn't a ship wonderful?' When they finally got off the ship, Marjorie found the harbour, like harbours the world over, was busy and noisy with everyone shouting in a language she didn't then understand. Soon all three of them, along with Marjorie's luggage, were put into a horse-drawn carriage and there began her real introduction to the India she soon learned to love. As they drove down the bazaar streets, the fragrance of spices mingled with the scent of leather, and the aroma from the coffee stalls surrounded her. The air was soft and moist. As they drove along, they wound in and out among cows, goats, bullock carts, coolies carrying bundles on their heads, vendors calling out their wares and eventually arrived at the Bentinck School for Girls which was to be her home for the next 10 years. She was immediately taken to a large old house and led up a long flight of semi-

Marjorie in the early days at the Bentinck School for Girls in Madras

circular stairs which led to a wide verandah facing out over a gathering of school girls waiting eagerly below. A large, fragrant garland of roses was placed over her head before she was turned around to face the students and was introduced. One of those girls, Florence Theophilus, only eight years old at the time, remembers it vividly: the first of many encounters in their lives.

Marjorie almost immediately felt drawn to the Indian way of life – its customs and its spiritual dimensions. The Madras school day began with prayer at 4.30 a.m. and for Marjorie this was a new

20

hint of what the fresh hour before dawn might offer. Night skies in India are like nowhere else in the world and at that season the Southern Cross shone brilliantly near. She found a new spiritual discipline in India's great tradition of silent meditation in the open air beneath the stars but felt she made 'only a stumbling, hesitant beginning'.

In those early days she also discovered another discipline in the emphasis on reverence for life. It was easy there to become completely vegetarian, so that possible barriers to an exchange of hospitality were removed. As the years went by she felt this was the right way for her, although it was never a rigid rule. But later both Tagore and Gandhi helped her to see that the real moral choice is between greed and self-restraint in eating any kind of food. Perhaps this is why friends with whom she has stayed over the years are able to report that when her vegetarianism would cause inconvenience to her hostess, she ate what was served without comment because as she said: 'Human relationships are more important'.

It is not surprising that with Marjorie's social background and home experience she reacted negatively to the suggestion by the School Principal, Alice Varley, that she call at Government House to make herself formally known to the British Raj. 'Why on earth should I?' said Marjorie. 'If I went to teach in London, I wouldn't go calling at Buckingham Palace!' 'Well,' said Alice Varley, 'one gets invitations to a garden party and other functions.' Marjorie replied that she could very well do without them and never did call. From then on neither did Alice.

It was a blessing for Marjorie that she joined Bentinck School when Alice Varley was Principal. Alice, at University College, London, had also come under the sway of the strong Student Christian Movement (SCM) that was such an influence on Marjorie at Cambridge, 15 years later. Alice's mentor was Frank Lenwood who contributed a great deal to making the SCM the creative force that it became in the universities. An article that he wrote in the SCM Journal, after a trip to India, moved Alice especially. He maintained that the aim of the missionary should be to enrich both Christian and non-Christian communities by a true mutual sharing of religious experience and this could only come through real and equal personal friendships between foreigners and Indians. When Marjorie arrived in Madras, she found Alice already putting these ideas into practice. This was the beginning of a 40-year friendship between the two of them.

Alice soon introduced Marjorie to the Madras International Fellowship founded by A. A. Paul, an Indian Christian who wanted to put into practice Gandhi's conviction that differences of opinion about politics or religion need not and should not prevent people from enjoying each other's company as fellow human beings. There were Indian members of several religions and political opinions and English members in business, education or government service, equally varied. They played together, enjoyed snacks together, and listened to one another with growing understanding and mutual respect. Marjorie learned a lot about India from them and many personal friendships started there.

The Fellowship held a weekend conference to which Marjorie went. There she first came in contact with Chakravarti Rajagopalachari (Rajaji) who was the main speaker. He told of Gandhi's constructive social reform programme which he himself was putting into practice at his own *Ashram* at Tiruchengode in the Salem District of South India. There began a friendship between Marjorie and Rajaji that was to influence her deeply. Rajaji was outstanding both intellectually and in his moral and spiritual stature. He later became the last Governor General of India, between the Declaration of Independence in 1947 and the adoption of the new constitution in 1950. That was, of course, later on, but there in Madras in the late '20s and early '30s when Marjorie herself was in her middle twenties, he was, as it were, her Guru in introducing her to the ideas of India – especially in the fields of politics and public affairs. Marjorie soon visited his ashram and found there a group of devoted people living together by a simple rule and serving the nearby villages in the spirit of Gandhi. It was the first ashram that Marjorie ever visited. They were having trouble because they were all working together there with no caste distinctions – Brahmins and untouchables all working together – drawing water from the same well, cooking together in the same kitchen. This so upset the villagers nearby that they refused to give them milk from their cows. Eventually, though, the villagers learned to appreciate the service given to them by those in the ashram.

One of Marjorie's fellow teachers, Rani Joseph, the Vice-Principal, had recently visited Tagore's school at Santiniketan and on her return taught the children of Bentinck, Tagore's song *Jana-gana-mana* – one verse of which later became India's National Anthem. The two verses quoted below in English translation first gave Marjorie a feel for the breadth of Tagore's vision:

> Thou art the ruler of the minds of all people
> Thou Dispenser of India's destiny
> Thy name rouses the hearts of the Punjab, Sind,
> Gujarat and Maratha, of Dravid, Orissa and Bengal.
> It echoes in the hills of the Vindhyas and Himalayas,
> Mingles in the music of Jumna and Ganga,
> And is chanted by the waves of the Indian Sea.
> They pray for Thy blessing and sing Thy praise,
> Thou Dispenser of India's destiny,
> Victory, Victory, Victory to Thee.
>
> Day and night, Thy voice goes out from land to land,
> Calling Hindus, Buddhists, Sikhs
>   and Jains round Thy throne
> And Parsees, Muslims and Christians.
> Offerings are brought to Thy shrine by
>   the East and the West
> To be woven in a garland of love.
> Thou bringest the hearts of all peoples
>   into the harmony of one life,
> Thou Dispenser of India's destiny,
> Victory, Victory, Victory to Thee.

In April 1930 Alice Varley married Ted Barnes, Professor of Chemistry at Madras Christian College. She was succeeded briefly as Principal by Rani Joseph who also left to be married, and Marjorie was appointed Principal. With her love of India and the Indian way of life and her ability at that time to converse easily in Tamil with the other staff members and to feel at one with them, she was an ideal person to undertake the work. A former student writes, 'Miss Sykes is remembered and loved as the daughter of England whose roots are embedded in the soil of India'. Her own approach is shown in the advice she gave many years later to the present Head Mistress, Mrs Prema Massillamani,

> It is not what we do but what we are that counts. And the quality does not depend on health or words, but only on the inward spirit and the grace of God.

A former pupil recalls, 'Miss Sykes taught four of us, sisters, English. She taught us to write correct English in simple sentences and encouraged us to do our best. In the High School classes we were given assignments which we were to do on our own. In the

Marjorie with her colleagues Kezie and Bala, Bentinck School for Girls in Madras

mornings we had classes and were given the afternoon to do our assignments under supervision. I personally liked this method. . . . It helped me to think hard and find answers to the problems in mathematics'. Not all of Marjorie's methods were academic. English and music together were enlivened by singing with the proper motions: 'John Brown's baby had a cold upon his chest and they rubbed it with camphorated oil'!

Meanwhile, Marjorie was impressed by the distinguished Indian women who came out of their homes (very unusual in those days for an Indian woman) to be part of the non-cooperation movement of 1930. She and her fellow teachers set to work to try to help the school girls become women of similar courage and dignity. They did this by emphasising cooperation instead of competition and abolished prizes. The quicker children were encouraged to help the slower ones, and the children of all classes swept and cleaned the buildings and compound. Sometimes their parents objected, saying that they sent their daughters to school to study, not to sweep floors and water plants. Others, though, including some of the national leaders of the city, deliberately chose to send their daughters there because of what the school was trying to do. Although English was taught in Bentinck and used for teaching the seniors classes, the younger children's understanding was limited. Marjorie invited women who were engaged in public service to talk to the children about their work and asked them to speak in Tamil. They often resisted this, feeling that, having been educated themselves in English medium schools, they would make grammatical errors in Tamil, but Marjorie usually persuaded them to agree.

All this was possible because Bentinck was a relatively small school – fewer than 350 children from kindergarten to final class – the teachers and children knew one another and cared for one another like a big family. The climate was always warm, furniture minimal and sandals rarely worn. Teachers and children alike went about barefoot and slept on grass mats on the floor; one small box held all a child's clothing and personal articles. Children of any religion or caste – high or low – were admitted on equal terms and treated in the same way. Resident children ate the same food from the same kitchen, regardless of caste. Local children brought their mid-day meal and sat down to eat it in little circles under the trees. One day Marjorie looked out and saw a senior Brahmin student clean away some used leaf plates left lying around by her careless low-caste juniors. Then she realised with a thrill that Gandhi's principles were taking hold of a new generation.

Although Marjorie was already familiar with many of Gandhi's principles and acting on them, the full impact of his educational programme struck her forcibly in August 1937. That day influenced her whole future life. She describes it thus:

> That August day in 1937 began like any other school working day, with classes to be taught and office work to be done. When the mail arrived, personal letters were put aside to be read later. I went to my room after lunch, taking them with me. Among them was my copy of *Harijan*, dated the 31st July, and when I began to turn its pages, a short paragraph caught my eye – Gandhiji's first public description of the kind of education *he* would like to see made available to children in India. Those few sentences drove everything else out of my mind. I was excited, I read them again and again, and I still remember clearly the words that came into my head: 'Here is someone talking real sense about education at last!' I looked eagerly for the next *Harijan*, and the next, and followed the controversies which Gandhiji's proposals had aroused. I read also of the plan to call selected educationalists together for a preliminary discussion that October. I had not met Gandhiji then, I was young and shy, and knew nothing of India except the South. So it never occurred to me, in spite of my enthusiasm, to invite myself into that meeting. I know now that I would have been welcome, but I have no regrets. Things worked out for me in another way.

In addition to carrying on the ideals already established, she also made many improvements in the physical arrangements of the school. As a part of the Centenary Celebration of the school (1937), four cottages for the school boarders were built, two on each side of a central open space, at one end of which a school chapel was built in 1932 in the pattern of an Indian *Mandapam*, open on three sides. The girls could walk straight to the chapel from their cottages to attend services. They sat on the floor on mats.

In 1988 the school built a new block to be named after Marjorie. It was Timothy Dawson, a civil engineer, the son of one of

Marjorie's first students back in 1929, who was selected to build the new building.

It was through the International Fellowship that Marjorie first met Quakers and very soon felt that this was where she belonged. She found that Quakers believed that an essential part of the way of Jesus was that peace, justice and righteousness should be expressed in practical living – ideas that had so attracted her at Cambridge. She responded to the Quaker belief that in all human beings of whatever race or creed, there is something that enables them to recognise and respond to 'Truth', 'a Light within', 'an inward teacher'.

When Alice married Ted Barnes, he was already part of a small Quaker group who met in each other's homes and Alice attended with him. Marjorie also began attending. There she experienced the depth of the silence in the Meeting for Worship. When asked in later years what drew her to Friends, she replied:

> My own growth in understanding of the Quaker way took place in this Indian context, alongside a growth in the under- standing of people whose religious roots were very different from my own. . . . As we sat together the outward silence deep- ened into inward stillness and a loving unity which might or might not find expression in simple spontaneous words. This was a different spiritual discipline from individual morning meditation but the practice of each kind of stillness helped the other kind immensely.

Those who met together in each other's homes there in Madras were mostly British, with a few Indians and one Dane. One of them, a Quaker Architect, Reginald Dann, especially impressed Marjorie. He earned his living in the Department of Town Planning in Madras but gave much of his time voluntarily to designing buildings for other groups. One of his most beautiful buildings is the chapel of Women's Christian College. He combined two major aspects of Quaker life – the concern for society expressed in his town plan- ning and the concern that reaching out to God should be expressed in buildings for worship. When Marjorie returned to England on furlough for the first time (1936), she became formally a member of the Religious Society of Friends and it has been an essential part of her life ever since.

Quakers also played an important part in the next stage of Marjorie's life. Although the 10 years at Bentinck School had been very happy ones and the freedom of encounter between members of the various religious communities in Madras very enriching, the effect of the Government of India Act of 1935 was to limit those freedoms. This Act provided for separate electorates for religious minorities and, in those circumstances increased numbers meant increased political clout. Suspicion, often wholly unjustified, took the place of open trust between religious communities and this meant that person-to-person exchange of ideas, previously so enriching became very difficult. That along with increasing government control of education made Marjorie feel the need for a more independent situation.

In the Autumn of 1938, H. G. Wood, a British Quaker who was visiting from England, came to Madras. He had recently met Tagore and told Marjorie of the poet's interest in having some 'representative of English culture' on his staff at Santiniketan, his great educational and social experiment in Bengal. He urged her to get in touch.

During her Christmas holiday she went on what she referred to as a 'pilgrimage' – first to Gandhi's school at Sevagram and then on to Santiniketan. That December of 1938 was a landmark in Marjorie's life. 'Within a few crowded days I came face to face with two of the greatest men then living – Mahatma Gandhi and Gurudev Rabindranath Tagore – and was welcomed and put wholly at my ease by the warmth of their courtesy.' In her later book *Gandhi: His Gift of the Fight* she tells of her memory of those days:

> These pictures are full of children. Children skipped and danced around Gandhi on his evening walks; they clung to his hands and chuckled at his jokes. Gandhi himself was absorbed and relaxed; for that half-hour he gave himself up completely to his delight in the children. That first evening Marjorie saw . . . a man who carried the burdens of the Indian people on his shoulders through a 16-hour working day, yet emerged at the end of it with all the zest and freshness of youth, apparently 'without a care in the world'. . . . The roots of that ever-renewed youthfulness went deep; one of its fruits was the quality of spirit which enabled him to become so happily and humbly a child among the children.

The school children
were bubbling over with life and happily busy. They kept the little mud-walled building and its surroundings scrupulously clean, they spun their yarn, singing old songs and learning new ones as they did so; they practiced the writing and counting and calculations that went into keeping their daily diaries and the records of their work. Piles of freshly picked cotton were drying in the sun, to be ginned and carded later.

This whole experience influenced Marjorie immensely in her own teaching.

When she went to Santiniketan a few days later, she found Tagore also surrounded by children. The 'eternal child' in the ageing poet responded to their interests and joys and set them free to 'do their own thing'. Tagore had started his school because he was in complete rebellion against the kind of education that he had suffered from as a little boy and which he saw still going on around him on all sides. Here he could develop his own ideas with complete freedom since the school was completely independent of government control. There was no tying down to examinations and very little to time tables. This was the kind of educational opportunity Marjorie had dreamed of and when Tagore warmly invited her to join his staff, and Friends Service Council in London made it possible financially for her to undertake the work, she accepted with enthusiasm.

CHAPTER FOUR

Santiniketan with Tagore 1939-41

MARJORIE JOINED THE STAFF at Santiniketan as 'representative of English Culture' early in July of 1939. On arrival she was taken to Tagore's room. There he was – once more surrounded by children who were coming in to greet him as they returned from their holidays. Tagore had tucked away under his chair and hidden behind his robe, a big tin of sweets. Every child received a handful and so did Marjorie !

She was soon installed in her own little three room brick house and began trying to get a garden to grow around it. Students from Kala-Bhavan, the art school of Santiniketan, came to study the flowers and paint frescoes around the verandah. She soon found the days full – teaching, learning Bengali, making friends.

'Santiniketan' had its beginning when Rabindranath's father, *Maharsi* (great saint) Devendranath Tagore, found under old trees on a wide upland, an experience of the presence and peace of God that ended his search for a place of retirement and meditation. A worn stone seat under two gnarled and twisted old trees in the centre of the Ashram has carved in it, in Bengali, the words: 'He is the repose of my life, the joy of my mind, the peace of my spirit'.

The Ashram is located 100 miles north-west of Calcutta and is set in a grove of stately sal trees from which one looks out on widely undulating country with high distant hills to the north. As Rabindranath Tagore wrote: 'In such surroundings, the ancient forest dwellers of India realised the spirit of harmony with the universe'. In 1901 he had asked and received the Maharsi's permission to create a school there where children might grow up to feel

The Poet and a Class under the trees at Santiniketan

Morning Prayers in front of the Library, Santiniketan

this spirit of harmony. By 1939 the school had grown into an international university. The place was still filled with Tagore's creativeness of spirit. New songs poured forth from him every morning and one of Marjorie's young women students, who had a quick musical ear, would often be called to record the melody before it

31

faded from his mind. Frail though he now was, he entered with youthful zest into the doings of the young people around him.

The children learned much through crafts like weaving and wood carving, as well as through music and drama. Marjorie, herself, had been much interested in putting on little plays for her friends when she was a child and responded with joy to the dramas great and small which were produced continually. It was a regular custom that one class should entertain the whole community with a presentation of what they had done in their class – a little drama, some music, some dancing, some recitation. They decorated the stage, wrote the programme and welcomed the guests – all was done by the children themselves, and became a natural unit of their education.

In Santiniketan Marjorie found once more the freedom of religious dialogue which had been cut short in Madras. Colleagues and older students were eager to exchange ideas and experiences. One thing they talked about was the differences between Indian and Western thought in the attitude towards history. For Western thought historical events formed a linear movement towards a consummation at 'the end of time'. Indian thought was of vast cosmic cycles in which particular events might have meaning only for their own world-age.

As time went by Marjorie found that there were many contributions that she could make to the general welfare. The fact of her presence made possible things that would not have happened otherwise. As a woman she could help the young women students in various ways. Her home was a place where Christian students and others who wished might meet on Sunday evenings for simple Christian worship. There were usually up to a dozen people present and great unity of spirit. Both girls and boys, began to drop in to talk about their religious perplexities and borrow books about religion or read the London Quaker journal, *The Friend*. Perhaps one day, she thought, when she had acquired enough Bengali, she might be asked to share occasionally in the leadership of the Wednesday morning worship service for the whole community. Sometimes those who conducted it, scholars as they were, were apt to talk over the heads of their young listeners. Marjorie knew that she could interest the children. She knew that this would take time, it depended on mutual friendship and trust, delicate intangible things whose growth cannot be hurried.

Other Quakers in India, and young missionary and Indian Christian friends, sometimes visited her at Satiniketan. She met others on train journeys and elsewhere, and when they discovered that she was working along-side others in Santiniketan with no feeling of compromising her faith, her fellow travellers often began talking of 'the things that are eternal'. She shared her religious experience with others, and they with her, as friend to friend.

In Santiniketan, time was set aside each day for meditation and worship in which everyone from the most learned scholar to the tiniest child took part. Every morning early everyone assembled in the open, shady place outside the library – girls on one side, boys on the other, little ones in front standing with the palms of their hands placed together in the attitude of worship. A short Sanscrit prayer of invocation and adoration was chanted in unison. Then came silence, a five minute silence, and then the invocation of peace. In the evening at sunset the bell rang again. All sat down quietly, wherever they happened to be, for another five minutes of recollection.

The sense of peacefulness was suddenly shattered in September of 1939 when news came that Britain had declared war on Germany. Marjorie described her own feelings as she sat alone on her verandah, 'while the sun set in the most wonderful pageantry of colour I ever remember to have seen. As it slowly faded, I looked with dread into the world darkness ahead'. A little 'peace group' which she had started earlier took on a new meaning.

It was at this point that Charles Freer Andrews came home to Santiniketan after a long absence. Marjorie had first met him when she visited England in 1936 and had shared discussions about India at a student conference. An Anglican priest who had first gone to India in his thirties, he was for more than a quarter of a century the closest English friend of both Tagore and Gandhi – known as the 'hyphen' between them. He had done much to prepare the ground for Gandhi's visit to the UK at the time of the Round Table Conference of 1931 and had stayed on afterward as Gandhi's interpreter. He was also admired the world over for ending indentured labour.

Now he was coming home, in failing health but still with his radiant faith, and was a great support to all of them as they struggled with the darkness of war. He soon formed the habit of dropping into Marjorie's house for a cup of tea as he returned from his early morning walk. Marjorie also formed the habit of dropping in on him later in the day to see if she could help him in any way – usually with his correspondence. Their friendship grew.

There were many links between Tagore and Gandhi and much coming and going between their two centres and in February of 1940 after an interval of many years Gandhi visited Santiniketan. Many students who did not normally wear *khadi* went out and bought white khadi clothes especially for the occasion. Marjorie, who normally wore only khadi, was incensed and felt that somehow truth was being compromised. She reacted by digging out and wearing the only non-khadi garment she possessed, a brilliantly coloured handloom sari which was very conspicuous in the white-clad crowd. She herself realised then that she had much to learn about 'non-violence of the spirit' and that she needed to learn to refrain from judging the inner motives of other people!

Early in April 1940, Andrews died in Calcutta. Marjorie, asked by Tagore to go to give him in person his loving messages, was with him almost to the end when she tore herself away to take the last train back to report to Tagore the news of his impending death. News of his actual death preceded her and they all mourned together. There was a service of prayer in the Mandir when Tangore spoke of his friend and asked Marjorie to translate what he had said into English. This translation verbatim from the Bengali of Tagore's tribute was used as the foreword to Andrew's last book, *The Sermon on the Mount*. The completed manuscript of this book which he had written earlier while in a hospital in Delhi, was found on his writing table in Santiniketan after his death.

As Marjorie walked back from Tagore's house that day, on the way to her own cottage, she suddenly felt the presence of her beloved father who had been such an influence in her life and realised that he, too, had just died and had come to say 'goodbye'. It was a most moving moment, deep grief but a sense of comfort too.

During the following summer, Marjorie spent her vacation studying Bengali in a language school in Darjeeling. The Tagore family spent their holiday in Kalimpong, not far away and Marjorie went over for Guruduv's birthday. (Gurudev means 'revered teacher', the name by which he was always called at Santiniketan.) In spite of the celebration, there was an underlying sadness. It was May of 1940 and news was continually coming through of the invasion of the small freedom-loving countries of western Europe.

Tagore had cherished friends in all these countries and in Germany itself. He was stunned and overwhelmed with grief – both for his friends and for all that this meant to the world.

It was then that Marjorie and Tagore came into a new relationship. Marjorie remembers that he almost physically shook himself free and said 'I'm doing no good at all sitting here moping. This is not the right way. What I should be doing is continuing to contribute what I can. What I can do is write, and I'm going to start once more writing down some of my memories of my own childhood – something universal, something human'. He called a little boy and sent him into the bazaar to buy an ordinary children's school exercise book. When he got it, out came his pen and he said to Marjorie, 'When I've finished writing this, I want you to put it into English'. He had liked her translation of his talk of C. F. Andrew's memorial service and wanted her to help him again. Later, back at Santiniketan, this notebook was sent along to Marjorie's house. He had written on one side of the page only, leaving the opposite side blank. He had a beautifully clear Bengali handwriting, so, fortunately Marjorie didn't have any problems with the actual reading. She found the work was great fun for an amusing pattern developed. Every now and then a messenger, usually a child, would appear saying 'Please, Gurudev would like that book back. He has thought of something else'. So the book went back. When it returned, it had all kinds of additions, subtractions and alterations. This went on right through until the English translation, apparently finished, duly appeared in the Santiniketan magazine. But then, later, when the Bengali version was published, it was found that Tagore, continually creative, had made yet more changes and additions, and the English version had to be re-done to match.

One day when this work was finished, Tagore asked Marjorie to undertake something very different – a translation into English of three plays he had written earlier, inspired by the teachings of the Buddha and by Gandhi's call to a non-violent struggle for freedom: *Chandalika*, *Natir Puja*, and *Mukta-dhara*. Marjorie was very aware of her inadequacy but felt that she could not refuse to try because she was so much convinced of the importance of those plays. She received generous help in the translation from her Indian friends and fellow workers. *Chandalika* was based on an old Buddhist legend – its heroine an 'untouchable' girl whom a Buddhist monk treats as a human being, and so reveals to her the dignity of her own humanity. *Natir Puja* was the story of the dancing girl who

35

comes to realise that her dancing is itself the best gift she can offer to the Lord, purified as it was by the love of her heart though others called it sacrilege. Marjorie found it 'the most difficult translation I have ever tackled just because the Bengali is so simply and naturally beautiful. One despairs of recapturing the freshness of its phrasing in English'. *Mukta-dhara* (The Waterfall Set Free) celebrated Tagore's own deep faith in freedom and expressed his political convictions with directness and force. The translation of this play made a great impression on Marjorie. Later on in Madras, she shared her translation with students in South India in the midst of the 'Quit India Movement' of 1942. It was only later that she discovered how much suspicion she had aroused in the minds of British authorities.

She went to spend a couple of weeks of her vacation in May 1941 in the Shevaroy Hills of South India with Ted and Alice Barnes. On the day that she arrived Ted became seriously ill with malignant malaria; pneumonia set in and three weeks later he died. Marjorie was able to help Alice with the nursing care and to be with her afterward during the difficult return to Madras to dismantle and store the contents of their little home. When that was done she and Alice spent 10 days of healing beauty together in the lovely, cool Nilgiri Hills. Marjorie wrote at the time:

> It has been supremely good thus to be where I was needed, and very wonderful to look back and see the guiding hand of God in the very hesitant and step-by-step decisions that went into the planning of that visit to the South, and made it easy to change my plans at short notice.

When Marjorie returned to Santiniketan, she found Tagore growing weaker and weaker. He had celebrated his 80th birthday in May receiving telegrams and letters from all over the world, but he was already seriously ill. Marjorie, in her later biography of Tagore for young people, describes his last weeks: 'All through the hot weather of 1941 faithful friends nursed him and did everything possible for his comfort. In July it was decided that he must go to Calcutta for treatment there and one morning the whole *Ashrama* assembled sadly in silence at the gates of his house to say goodbye to him. As the car moved slowly away they sang to him the Santiniketan song. In Calcutta everything possible was done to save his life, but in vain. On 7th August, 1941, he died, very peacefully

36

and quietly, in the old Jorasanko house where he had been born and his body was cremated in the evening at the Nimtola Ghat by the Ganges'. His friends like to remember some of his words written earlier when he thought about his own death:

At this time of parting, wish me good luck, my friends. The sky is flushed with the dawn and my path lies beautiful.

CHAPTER FIVE

Women's Christian College, Madras 1941-44

DURING THE MONTHS after Tagore's death, Marjorie felt the need of a break. Alice Barnes came to Santiniketan for Christmas 1941 and then she and Marjorie set out for Hoshangabad for a gathering of scattered Friends. On the way they stopped in Benares (Varanasi) to visit a friend, and Marjorie became involved in helping harvest tomatoes in the hot sun. After they reached Hoshangabad she developed a low fever, and Martin Ludlam, the Quaker doctor at Itarsi, put her in the hospital there for observation.

After the war broke out, Marjorie had been trying to keep scattered, lonely pacifists in India in touch with one another for mutual support and encouragement. Some of her letters were intercepted, and the police arrived at the hospital to interview her. Edith Bevan, the English nursing superintendent, who had come to India about the same time as Marjorie did in 1928, told the police very forcefully: 'No one can interview patients in *my* hospital unless I permit it – and I don't!' They meekly departed!

Marjorie's illness was diagnosed as exhaustion and she was given a three months' leave of absence from Santiniketan. She went home with Alice Barnes to Coimbatore and there in that peaceful atmosphere began to recover her energy. Alice had only lived there a short time and there was lots of pioneer work to be done in planning and making a garden. There were one or two other Friends in the town, so a little Meeting for Worship was started in Alice's home. It was a happy time but soon Marjorie was sufficiently recovered to want something to do that required more of her energy. There was a home for orphans at Kotagiri in the Nilgiri Hills where assistance was badly needed, and she went to help. She spent one interesting morning addressing a meeting of shrewd, intelligent Nilgiri farmers on the system of Health Cooperatives worked out at Sriniketan, the agricultural section of Tagore's university. Men from many villages in the Eastern half of the Nilgiris were there. They were Bagadas, fine agriculturists, and Marjorie re-furbished her Tamil among them and among the children.

In May 1942 Marjorie and Alice enjoyed a quiet, restful and friendly holiday in a delightful little cottage hidden among woods on a hill top. In this atmosphere Marjorie was able to start writing a life of Tagore for school children. By the middle of June, the first draft was done and in July she typed out and sent copies to people who knew the poet intimately and others who knew the standard of English of the school children, and aimed with their help to have the book ready for a publisher by Christmas. She wanted large sales and wide publicity – not in order to make money, but so that children all over India might read about the poet's life and ideals. The book, *Rabindranath Tagore*, was accepted and published by Orient Longmans in 1943. Since then it has been translated into many Indian languages and is still being sold.

Meanwhile, a message had come from Miss Rivett, the Principal of Women's Christian College in Madras, saying that they were desperate for a teacher of English, since war conditions made it impossible for replacements to come out from England. Would Marjorie come? Santiniketan was consulted and agreed to loan her to Women's Christian College for two years from July 1942. She agreed to go only if she could live off campus and carry out her concern for living in a poor section of the city and being part of a natural community.

Miss Rivett had the vision to see how Marjorie's desire might fit into a creative pattern already established. For many years, students had spent Friday evenings in social service in 'Mohammedan's Gardens', a crowded hutment area, where they played with the children and encouraged clean habits. They realised that this short weekly contact had its limitations and were looking for a way to be more effective. If Marjorie could find a home in that area, she could study the situation and try to work something out.

During the first term, however, Marjorie lived in the college. It was a time of great political stress, because of the sudden unexpected arrest of Gandhi and other Congress leaders. In the Women's Christian College feelings were first expressed in a spontaneous 24 hour fast of mourning. Then the feelings began to grow that a strike, in which they united with other Madras students, was a necessary public expression of their feelings. The strike came, but the college was divided; a strong minority did attend classes. The staff regarded themselves as responsible to both parties. They taught fragments of classes whose minds were clearly elsewhere, supplied strikers with books on national problems to read during the time at their disposal, and organised a study of Gandhi's 'constructive programme' in which *all* could unite. They also held services of worship and intercession attended by almost the whole college. After a week, the strike leaders came to the Principal to say that they felt that the strike should now end, and to ask that the college should be closed early for the coming vacation. The staff at once agreed. Both sides were worn out, they could not possibly

View of the Courtyard and Chapel at Women's Christian College, Madras

Interior view of the Chapel at Women's Christian College, Madras

write examinations then. Before the students left, they elected a National Service Committee to make plans for constructive service when they returned. One of the results was a 'Grow More Food' campaign which meant hard work in making a vegetable garden behind their hostel, and diverting their bath water to irrigate it. Marjorie had a hand in this project, and it *was* productive.

In September there was a small Japanese air raid on the city; many frightened slum dwellers ran away, back to their village homes and one of the houses in Mohammedan's Gardens became available. There were a few small brick and tile houses and many thatched huts crowded together. Marjorie moved in on 20th October, 1942 and Horace Alexander, British Quaker and close friend of Gandhi, was the first guest to be welcomed. Donald Groom, Director of the Friends Rural Centre, Rasulia, Mid-India, came in November as the first overnight guest. The house was close to a maidan at one end of the slum. It had three tiny rooms on the street side and a narrow verandah open to the courtyard behind with a kitchen at one end. Marjorie added a bathroom and a toilet in a corner of the courtyard which was enclosed with a wall.

Florence Theophilus, who as a child of eight had seen Marjorie arrive at Bentinck school, was now a Demonstrator in the College in the Department of Home Science, the Head of which was Dr Eleanor Mason. Marjorie had known Eleanor since her first days in India when they became good friends and remained so over the years. There was no accommodation for Florence Theophilus in the college and she had a long and tiring daily journey from her own home, so Marjorie invited her to share her new found home. Their kitchen became the scene of many interesting experiments in tasty and low-cost nutritious diets.

The Christmas holidays that year (1942-43) were some of the happiest Marjorie ever spent. She went straight back to Santiniketan for nine days, and greatly enjoyed getting to know Abanindranath Tagore, the poet's distinguished artist nephew. There was the usual Christmas morning service in the open air under the mango trees. The beloved and respected Bishop of Calcutta, in a message for people at large, had written a beautiful plea for all who felt themselves wronged in any way, to take the initiative in seeking reconciliation and offering service. Marjorie felt privileged in being asked to read this message at the close of her own short talk.

Earlier there had been a severe cyclonic storm in Southwest Bengal where a tidal wave had broken through the coastal embankment and destroyed mile upon mile of ripening rice and thousands of cattle. The Friends Ambulance Unit (FAU) was at work in the worst affected area, and after her Santiniketan holiday Marjorie went to help. She held the fort there for a few days until two Bengal ladies came to relieve her. Then she travelled back for another four days in Santiniketan, where she reintroduced Horace Alexander on his first visit to the school after 15 years.

When Marjorie and Florence Theophilus returned from their holidays, they had a new concern. They found that most of their neighbours – both husbands and wives – went out for daily work. The day began at 4 a.m. when a man would bring a handcart to the street corner and sell hot coffee (made from the discarded coffee-grounds of the hotels) at one anna (about 1½p) a cup. Men drank it and went off on their cycles to work in distant parts of the city. The women took their waterpots to the nearest public tap (so did Marjorie and she soon learned the local art of wedging the tap with a stone, so that her second pot would be filled while she carried home the first!). Hastily they swept and cooked, and then they too went to work. Their older children, especially if they were girls, did not go to the school nearby. It was more important for them to look after the babies and toddlers while the mothers worked. What was needed, it seemed, was a nursery school where the little ones might be cared for while the older children went to school. Marjorie and Florence put this proposal before the college students and asked if they would guarantee Rs. 400 for a teacher's salary and the cost of a year's trial.

The students were enthusiastic and a trained nursery school teacher was found. She also became a member of the family in the little house. Lack of a building did not trouble them. After breakfast, Marjorie and Florence, Women's Christian College teachers, would go off to college and Jayamani, the nursery school teacher, would visit the houses, collect the children and take them to the house. Soon she had 20 children. They had stories and handwork in the cheerful brick floored 'study room'. They played singing games in the courtyard and sometimes went out on the maidan. At

43

mid-day they lined up on the verandah for a meal of 'ragi balls', sprouted green gram and buttermilk, and Marjorie would cycle home from college to share it with them. In the evening when they had gone home, the room became a 'study room' once again.

The Nursery School grew until a separate building was needed to house it, but by that time Marjorie had gone back to Bengal and Jayamani had left to be married. Mrs Rani M. Dawson (neé Simon), who had once been Marjorie's pupil at Bentinck, and later her colleague at Women's Christian College, tells how this was accomplished:

> All the other staff members of Women's Christian College contributed for a fund to buy a piece of land in that slum area and build a regular nursery school. The students of Women's Christian College, not to be behind-hand in this project, put on a public entertainment to raise funds from the sale of tickets, to pay the salary of a regular nursery-trained teacher who would work in the new nursery school building which was now named 'MacDougall Memorial Nursery School' after our first Principal of Women's Christian College.

The students continued to contribute to the salary of the teacher in the following years. Today this project has expanded into a regular Government recognised nursery school with Government grant, Kindergarten classes, mid-day meal plan and other benefits.

Marjorie was able to attend its Silver Jubilee Celebration held in 1973. She protested, jokingly, that this was merely the Jubilee of the *building*, not of the school, which by 1973 had been in existence for 30 years. After the meeting a smiling young man approached, who 30 years earlier had been a toddler in that first group in 1943. Now he had with him his own little daughter.

Florence Theophilus shares her own memories of those early days:

> I am glad I had the opportunity to live with Marjorie Sykes in her house as I learnt a lot from her. First, dignity of labour. She, a professor, went to the street tap like the other women in that area, getting up at 4 a.m. every morning and thus made rapport with them. She talked with me about her experience in Santiniketan, about Rabindranath Tagore and C. F. Andrews. We had breakfast and supper together. Even though

44

I was once her pupil in Bentinck, she treated me as her equal when we both joined the Women's Christian College. I attended a meeting of 'Friends' (Quakers) arranged in our home. I experienced with them the periods of silence observed and a prayer or a verse in a hymn shared with the members. I understood the value of periods of quiet during the worship. We even had a small vegetable garden in the courtyard and grew radish and carrots and a few other vegetables. . . . We used our produce for our vegetable dishes. She taught us how to cook dry chappaties which we had for supper. We had only a firewood stove for cooking. Marjorie Sykes believed in simple living.

At some point during these years at Women's Christian College a series of events began which was to influence Marjorie's life considerably. In 1943 the women in charge of the orphanage in Kotagiri wrote that they felt anxious about a girl, called Nesamani, who had been 'adopted' by a family in Madras. Marjorie found that in fact she was being treated as a servant, but that for various reasons the family was quite willing to let her go. Since Florence had gone into residence in the college, there was room for Nesamani to join Marjorie and Jayamani in the little house. She was a famine orphan who had had a very bad start in life and perhaps for that reason was not very academically inclined. Marjorie sent her to a school nearby and she passed the fifth standard. Then she returned to Kotagiri to be trained as a children's nurse, work for which her affectionate nature made her very suitable.

Marjorie asked if there were any other children in the Kotagiri orphanage who could profit by more education. There was 13-year-old Rani, very small for her age, but clearly intelligent, who might benefit from a high school education which was not then available in Kotagiri. She was brought affectionately into Marjorie's home and became her daughter from then on. Marjorie sent her as a day student to the nearest Girls' High School. Several months after her arrival Marjorie wrote:

> She is a jolly member of the family, happy at school, making good progress. She has grown more than an inch in the last three months. There are tiny indications now and then that she is beginning to think independently about life and religion. These usually come out on the rare occasions when she

45

and I have been alone for our evening family prayers. When I think of the rather frightened, forlorn little person whom I first saw standing among the scurrying crowds at the Central Station one morning and look at her merry face now as she teases Jaya or gathers shells on the beach on one of our very rare picnics, I rejoice and give thanks.

Sunday, 24th September, 1944, was a day never to be forgotten by any of those involved. A number of travelling Friends converged on Madras: Christopher Taylor was passing through on his way from Malabar to take charge of the Friends Ambulance Unit (FAU) headquarters in Calcutta; Clem Alexandre going in the opposite direction to a well-earned holiday in Malabar; and Doris and Ranjit Chetsingh, who had started the Delhi Quaker Centre in 1943 were there to discuss Quaker concerns. The little Madras Meeting for Worship being thus swollen, and college being on vacation, they decided to have Meeting that Sunday morning in the College Chapel and not in Marjorie's little '10 by 10' room as usual. They were then to go over to Marjorie's home afterward for lunch and a quiet chat about the Delhi Centre and other matters of Quaker concern. Marjorie hurried home ahead of the others to help Rani with the final preparations for lunch.

I hadn't been home five minutes [wrote Marjorie in her Journal Letter to Friends Service Council] when there came simultaneously a great shout, a smell of something burning, and Rani's frightened cry 'House on Fire'! We looked up and saw beyond the wall of our tiny courtyard a great cloud of smoke that rolled towards us and burst into a sheet of flame as it rolled. The thatched roofs in the adjacent courtyards were soon alight and for a few minutes it looked as if our more solid house too was in danger. At any rate we hurried our more valuable and inflammable possessions across the street out of harm's way, while young village men mounted our bathroom roof and flung our water at the nearest burning hut. Their efforts and the fact that my succulent banana trees acted as most effective spark quenchers, stopped the fire in our direction, and meantime the fire engines had arrived and dealt with it in other areas. So when our guests arrived for their 'quiet meal', they found Rani sitting on our boxes in the street, me first-aiding a burnt arm, and the whole block of which our

46

house is one corner, cordoned off by the police and soused with water.

The homes of 31 families were reduced to a wreck of blackened, slippery mud, and over 110 people left with nothing but what they stood up in and in some cases a goat or two and a brass water pot. Luckily it was mid-day and animals were all out grazing. The fire once started in that bone-dry thatch spread with such ferocity that people could save nothing but themselves.

The little Quaker group ate the rice and greens which had already been prepared and retired to Marjorie's sitting room while some of the homeless cooked rice and dhal in Marjorie's kitchen. Marjorie lent out every mat, carpet, ground sheet and old sari that could be used to sleep on. The first night all slept in the open field. The second night a pathetic little procession came calling 'Amma, it's raining'. 'Then,' said Marjorie, 'our three little "10 by 10" rooms and the "five by 20" verandah held three dozen extra people of both sexes and all ages.' Marjorie and the recognised headman of the village held a meeting and made a list of the sufferers by families; and clothing, one garment each, was provided.

Problems arose because ration cards had been burned up and people could not get their rice.

The rationing officer himself [wrote Marjorie], was most helpful but he was unluckily out when I sent my messenger to receive new cards. The messenger was one of the poor sufferers, dressed (like Gandhi) in a loin cloth only; some snobbish little upstart clerk bullied him and sent him away empty handed. When he came back after nearly four miles walking in the blazing sun and stood patient and uncomplaining before me, I just blazed up. There ensued a hot telephone conversation (on the college phone) with that office, from which I emerged with triumph blended with my anger, having extracted a promise that the missing cards should be sent by special messenger. And when an hour later they were safely in my hands, and I was waving them joyfully at those of my colleagues who had witnessed the explosion of my wrath, a little half-mocking voice spoke up inside me in the words of the book of Jonah: 'Doest thou well to be angry?' And I answered with great conviction 'Yes, I do well to be angry –

47

being angry get things done!' and then began to wonder all the same whether it was *altogether* well??

What touches one most deeply in these crises [wrote Marjorie], is the cheerful, uncomplaining patience with which those who have so nearly nothing in this world endure the loss of their pitifully little all. And though I have sometimes during the last weeks been physically very weary indeed, I felt that my conviction of the value of living right among the ordinary folk would have been fully justified by this experience alone.

When Marjorie finished teaching at Women's Christian College and went back to Santiniketan in 1944, Rani came there on vacation, having been happy to stay in boarding at her school in Madras. She was soon in the kitchen pointing at different things and getting their names in Bengali, which she wrote down in Tamil script. It was clear that she was an intelligent and enterprising child. She had made up her mind to do nurses' training as soon as she had finished high school. She was the oldest child in her family, and could remember her parents. Her father had been a male nurse in Dr Somervell's great hospital in Neyyoor, Travancore and she was determined to follow in his footsteps. She went for training to a hospital in Madras which provided a nursing course, but that was not until later.

During these Madras years along with Rani, the village life, Quaker concerns, and the contact with students at Women's Christian College in class, in choir, in the college garden, and the debating society, there was a literary side to Marjorie's life.

The 'Hindu' newspaper occasionally asked Marjorie for a review of some book connected with Bengali or Bengal. A west-coast Christian Ashram asked her to contribute to its monthly journal a series of articles on 'some aspects of Quakerism, with special references to the features in it which might contribute to the Church in India'.

There was also the final revision and proof reading for her book on Tagore for young people. In her journal letter dated 13th February 1944 she was able to report that the book was well received and already being reprinted and being prescribed as a text book for public examinations in Madras and Ceylon (now Sri Lanka). A large beautiful volume of essays was compiled to be given to Gandhi on his 75th birthday in 1944. The book was called simply *Gandhiji* and Marjorie was asked to write a chapter on 'The Influence of Christian Thought on Gandhiji'.

In the midst of all the variety of responsibilities in Marjorie's life, she was able to write in one of her Journal Letters to the Friends Service Council:

> This 'business of living' becomes more and more 'this business of friendliness' with students, villagers, colleagues and a heterogeneous crowd of all sorts and conditions of people as the subject of it. The external routine goes on and on and is a necessary framework, but the real significance doesn't lie in that.

CHAPTER SIX

C. F. Andrews Biography 1944-49

AT THE END OF THE COLLEGE YEAR IN 1944, Marjorie returned to Santiniketan to work on the biography of Charles Freer Andrews in collaboration with Benarsidas Chaturvedi. There she held the Andrews Memorial Chair which allowed her to devote a large part of her time to the biography. Between 1944 and 1946 she was able to gather whatever information was available in India itself. One of the most important sources was Andrew's correspondence with Gandhi, and in 1945 Marjorie went to ask Gandhi if she might consult his files. Gandhi immediately agreed, and as there was still some time left of the five minutes she had been allotted, he then turned to her: 'Now let me ask *you* something; would *you* consider coming to help us with education? It would make us all very happy.' The invitation took Marjorie completely by surprise. 'But there is this biography to write,' she said, 'I'm committed to that.' 'I know you couldn't come *now*,' Gandhi replied, 'But if you yourself feel it to be right for you, come when you can.'

The next thing was to go to England to gather material there while there were still people alive who remembered Andrews in his younger days. She had not been able to go during the war and in 1946 it was still very difficult to get a passage. She tried and tried without success. Finally she got in touch with the Secretary for Education who understood the urgency of her problem and with his help she was able to get priority for a flight to England, and was instructed to be in readiness at Karachi.

She suddenly got a call to be at the dock at 4 a.m. to take off on a hydroplane (a flying boat which lands on water) which was on its way to England from China. She went out in a small boat, up a ladder, and there she beheld a Giant Panda with a block of ice to keep it cool, tucked away in the mail compartment. Its Chinese attendant was one of the passengers. They were en route to London, the Panda having been donated to the zoo by the Chinese Government.

The route was via Bahrain to Cairo where the plane landed on the Nile at dusk. When it took off again there was real luxury: seats were folded into the floor, beds were made up with sheets and blankets and released from the cabin walls and passengers slept in comfort. The next morning dawned in Sicily where roses and mulberries replaced the desert sands of the previous day's flight. Then on past Mt Etna, across Corsica and France to land in the wide harbour at Poole where the really important passenger, the panda, was received with due honours by a delegation of zoo keepers. Marjorie and her fellow human beings travelled by bus through the beauty of the New Forest in May to London. It was Marjorie's first experience of air travel and a very memorable one.

Apart from Andrews' surviving brother and sisters, Marjorie knew only one name, that of his clergyman friend, Outram, who in 1912 had given Tagore much needed rest in his country vicarage. Outram, she found, was still alive, caring for a little village church on the Devonshire coast not far from Bude. She wrote, received a warm invitation, and paid a very happy and rewarding visit. Outram not only had his own knowledge, he was also able to give her the names and addresses of a number of others who had known Andrews at school in Birmingham and during his years in Cambridge and London. Andrews' elder brother was equally helpful about the family background.

Agatha Harrison, Andrews' literary executor, was also a very great help, and Andrews' former publishers, George Allen and Unwin, were eager to have the opportunity to bring out his biography. Marjorie spent some time writing at Woodbrooke (the Quaker Study Centre near Birmingham) until 15th February of the Spring Term of 1947, and shortly afterwards returned to India to finalise it with her co-author, Benarsidas Chaturvedi. On 1st June, 1947, she wrote to Jack Hoyland back at Woodbrooke:

> Eleven chapters (half the total) of the Andrews book went off yesterday to Allen and Unwin and a duplicate to Agatha, four

51

more ready to go and waiting for their brothers to return from the final typing and be finally checked. It has taken longer than I hoped. Benarsidas Chaturvedi had found some valuable material in my absence which considerably modified one chapter; and then even the more mechanical job of checking typescripts is quite a job when every small correction must be put into five copies! I have been kept pretty hard at it ever since I returned to India, some 10 or 11 weeks now.

Marjorie and Benarsidas asked Gandhi for a Foreword. He responded gladly with a few short moving sentences. Horace Alexander thought they were *too* short, and asked him to expand them. It happened to be Gandhi's day of silence, so he pencilled his reply – 'What I wrote came from the heart'. It was left as Gandhi wrote it:

> Charlie Andrews was simple like a child, upright as a die, and shy to a degree. For the biographers the work has been a labour of love. A life such as Andrews' needs no introduction; it is its own introduction.

When the biography was finished, Marjorie was able to think of responding to the invitation which Gandhi had given her in 1945 to join his team at Sevagram and help with the educational programme. The first step was to see what had been done up to that time. During the war, most of the 'basic schools' which followed Gandhi's plan had been closed and the teachers arrested because the schools were considered centres of political propaganda. But in Bihar there had been friendly understanding between the Government Secretary of Education and the basic school teachers, and a group of village schools in a northern district had been able to work without interruption for seven or eight years. They had done fine work, and Marjorie was happy to be among them when they celebrated Independence Day on 15th August, 1947.

The happiness was soon clouded. A few days later there were riots in Calcutta. Gandhi was there fasting, trying to bring peace to the area. Marjorie, along with others, went there to see what she could do to help. Gandhi said there was plenty to do everywhere, and that each person should remain where their normal work was and work for non-violence there. Marjorie therefore went back to Madras to be with Rani, her daughter, during the final months before she entered nurses' training. Once more she worked at Women's Christian College, this time as Librarian. Her successor, Miss K. Ambika, recalls that Marjorie

> Classified and catalogued the entire collection of books according to the Dewey decimal system which she modified to suit Indian conditions. . . . The Library was her home ever afterwards and she used to spend hours working there during all her visits to Madras. She gave advice and suggestions regarding new books and she even suggested using Neem leaves (dried in the shade) for insecticide.

The idea of leaving India after Independence never occurred to Marjorie:

> I was 42, and had spent almost all my working life in India. By then, with my dark eyes and hair, sun-tanned skin and simple Indian dress, I was often mistaken for an Indian by birth. India was a second home, and when the new Constitution came into operation it was a great satisfaction to find that my 19 years of Indian domicile qualified me for citizenship without further formality. I have been an Indian citizen ever since.

CHAPTER SEVEN

Gandhi's Ashram at Sevagram 1949-59

RANI ENTERED NURSES' TRAINING SCHOOL in the summer of
1949 and Marjorie was then free to accept Gandhi's earlier invitation to join the Community at Sevagram. By that time Gandhi was
no longer there; he had been assassinated by a Hindu fanatic in
January 1948. Marjorie had been with friends in Bangladore when
the news came and the memory of the wordless kindness with which
they surrounded her has remained with her ever since.

Marjorie's responsibility at Sevagram was the training of teachers for the 'new education' (Nai Talim) started by Gandhi. Marjorie
describes this training in a letter to friends:

> Every year a new class of students is put down here, away from
> towns with their piped water and municipal lighting and sani-
> tation, in a settlement in the middle of village India. They are
> given houses to live in, a kitchen and dining hall, a workshop
> and some wells and fields. We say to them, 'Here you are . . .
> Grow your food, pick your cotton, spin yarn and weave your
> clothes, cook your meals, plan and care for your own sanitary
> system, keep your surroundings clean and hygienic and your
> buildings in repair. Tackle each of these jobs as intelligently
> and scientifically as you can; find out what sort of knowledge
> and skill you need to do them efficiently, and find out how
> you can get it. When you have re-educated yourself in REAL
> knowledge by these means, you will be ready to do your bit
> in the education of the nation.
>
> We teachers spend our days alongside the students in the
> field and kitchen and workshops, helping them with the tech-
> nique, with the organisation, with the recording, analysis and

study of their daily chores and with the machinery of responsible self-government that goes with it all. They are nearly all
completely new to it, and in the few months of their training
they cannot and do not produce one half or one quarter of
their own essential needs. But they do learn perhaps to
measure worth and knowledge by a new, realistic standard.

Side by side with the teachers' training school, whose
personnel changes from year to year, is the older, more stable
school community, where growing children are being
educated by these methods of self-reliance and intelligent
work. The two communities help each other and pool their
resources for emergencies and special needs (like harvesting).
But there are never enough workers here for all there is to do;
there are constant calls on us to help the new 'basic national'
schools and training centres in other parts of the country. And
therefore our programme is very heavy, and personal interests
outside the work tend to get crowded out. The days are not
long enough for all there is to do – we fall asleep before we
have finished. But if you believe, as I do, that Gandhiji was
fundamentally right in what he declared to be necessary for
human welfare, it is absorbingly interesting and worth-while.

In addition to her major responsibility, there was much variety
in the work Marjorie found to do as soon as she arrived. First there
was the reorganisation of the library. Then there was the weaving
which Marjorie herself was just learning. She found that only white
yarn was being used and she felt that the children needed colour
both for interest and because it was easier to count threads that
way. Much experimenting was done with colours from vegetable
dyes and the process of dyeing developed apace. The only place for
doing it, however, was an old kerosene tin perched on three stones
over a 'campfire' in a precarious patch of shade. When in 1951 a
big weaving shed was built ('Kabir-Bhavan' named for Kabir, the
weaver-poet-saint of India), plans were made for adding a section
for carding and dyeing.

Very soon after Marjorie's arrival there was an additional
responsibility. The World Pacifist Meeting for which Marjorie had
helped to plan while she was still in Madras, was held in two
sessions, the first at Santiniketan, the second after an interval, at
Sevagram. The idea for such a meeting had originated with Horace

Alexander who felt that steps should be taken to bring the pacifists of Western countries into touch with Gandhi and his followers in India for a world-wide movement of non-violence. Gandhi had welcomed the idea but wanted it postponed until after Independence. A preliminary All-India planing meeting was held at Rasulia, the Quaker Rural Centre at Hoshangabad, in January 1948. Gandhi's death came soon after. It was decided to have the conference even though the foreign visitors could no longer meet Gandhi, but it was postponed until December 1949. The opening meetings were held at Santiniketan in early December and after the delegates had travelled in India and Pakistan for almost two weeks, they re-convened at Sevagram on Christmas Eve when Dr Rajendra Prasad, as Chairman of the Meeting, broadcast from Sevagram an appeal for peace.

On Christmas night the Sevagram community under Marjorie's direction presented a simple and very moving Nativity Pageant in which members of the conference took part as Carol Singers. It is described in the report of the conference, *The Task of Peacemaking:*

> The pageant was held in . . . the cow-shed and lighted only by the subdued illumination of oil lanterns. All round the great yard were the stalls of 40 white cows, one of which appropriately gave birth to a calf in the middle of the Christmas ceremony. The Carol Singers stood amidst the cows singing 'Stille Nacht', 'Adeste Fidelis', and 'The First Noel'. Joseph and Mary went into real cow-sheds and the Child Jesus was laid in an actual manger. The shepherds came from the highlands of Ladakh on the Tibet border, and played their parts to perfection. Above the silent countryside the crescent moon and the vivid stars shone from a delicately clouded sky. The scene was probably as close an approximation to the traditional scene in Bethlehem as the modern world could achieve, and no one who took part in the pageant will ever forget it.

As to the conference itself, Marjorie describes her reaction to it in a letter to a friend:

> It *was* valuable but not so much for what it said as for the balls it set rolling and especially for the friendships and contacts made. Each of us treasures our address list and they are being used, I feel sure. Probably the most significant trend of thought

was the endorsement by the whole group, with only one exception, that the fundamentals of a peaceful world can only be reached by living in accordance with true *human* values and basing society on cooperative and creative *work* instead of on artificial money values – ie. by something of which 'Nai Talim' in India is one form of expression. Such ideas are struggling to birth in many different lands.

In this same letter Marjorie tells a bit more about her everyday life.

We live a crowded life. Apart from sheer learning the ropes, and the daily programme of the teacher training section, there are always things that command one's interest and attention. I am longing to do far, far more than I have managed to do yet about Basic Education *literature* and when this course ends this month, I shall get some chance. Many visitors, some very interesting ones, come for studying our ideas and methods; we have welcomed a whole batch of 'D.P.' (Displaced Persons) homeless and rootless children from Sind, and we are watching them grow into the community. And so on and so on. We are always under staffed but we manage to survive. . . . I expect to be in Madrass towards the end of April. Rani has her holiday then and I want to see something of her.

In addition to her responsibilities at Sevagram itself, Marjorie had periods of strenuous travelling – mostly visits of advice to Basic Training Schools or plans for starting them, along with some talks on Gandhian methods at educational conferences.

In July of 1950, Marjorie had a very anxious time when her adopted daughter, Rani, still a student nurse in Madras, suddenly fell unconscious, remaining so for 40 hours, and then had a series of epileptic-type convulsions. Marjorie took her to the well-known hospital in Vellore to be under the care of a brilliant neurologist there. In spite of a recurrence of the trouble in November, all of the most exhaustive tests were negative – leaving the diagnosis as some anxiety hysteria related to her concern for the welfare of her two younger sisters who were in an unsatisfactory orphanage. News that they might be brought out and the family reunited brought hope. Rani recovered; she and her brother brought their sisters home; and Rani's cure was permanent.

Rani completed her training and started on an independent nursing career. After a year or two it seemed time to consider marriage for her. She had an aunt in Trivandrum who was willing to help arrange the marriage according to the family's ideas. Rani, however, insisted that her younger sisters (who hadn't had her

Marjorie Sykes at Sevagram

chance of education) should be settled first, and with the help of her brother and her aunt that was happily done. A little later Rani indicated that *she* was now ready, and a marriage was arranged. This turned out very well and two little daughters were born to them.

At Sevagram in 1952 Marjorie and her students built her a house. There was a one-acre field a little way from the buildings – an acre that needed to be guarded. There was a well with a mound of earth beside it where a home could be built and Marjorie claimed it as the work project for her new class. Two of the men knew carpentry and another knew how to tile a roof. An ancient wattle and timber structure had been demolished and its doors, windows and timber could be used. A lot of happy team work followed, and a little house in the local village style arose. Then came the opening ceremony. As is the custom in India, milk must first be boiled in the house, and sweets served. So Marjorie moved in. Her first guest was Mrs Chester Bowles, the wife of the American Ambassador to India.

During the following years when Aryanayakam, the director of the whole programme, was showing government officials around, he would bring them past the house. As they approached he would ask them how much they would spend on a college Principal's house. 'About Rs. 20,000' they would reply. 'Well,' said he, 'here is ours – and it cost about Rs. 200.'

Meanwhile in March 1951 the Seventh All-India Basic Education Conference with 700 delegates met in the new weaving shed at Sevagram and Marjorie's life-long interest and talent in drama found new scope for expression. The students performed a dramatic pageant of Indian history which they called 'Bharat-Ki-Katha'. Marjorie writes:

> By dance and songs, by tableau and silent action we brought before the audience the whole sweep of history – from the primitive forest dwellers and tribes of the Stone Age, through the Dravidian and Aryan Cultures, the story of the great epics, the Buddhist, Christian, Muslim contributions to Indian Culture and traditions, down to the awakening of India in the 20th century at the call of Mahatma Gandhi.

The year 1952 saw the beginnings of university level education at Sevagram. The academic standards were high, but consciously

59

and specifically shaped to serve the needs of rural India in agriculture, animal husbandry, health, engineering, etc. At the same
time both staff and students were following with the deepest interest Vinoba Bhave's Bhoodan (Land Gift) Movement which had
begun in 1951. Parties of them began going out into the villages
around Sevagram and giving his message, as they were already going
out under Marjorie's direction to help the teachers and the children in the village schools.

Marjorie had a three months' leave of absence from Sevagram
in the summer of 1955 to do some writing connected with Basic
Education and a translation from French to English of Lanza de
Vasto's book *Gandhi to Vinoba*, which described the Bhoodan
Movement. She went up to the cool Nilgiri Hills and stayed at
Kotagiri with Alice Barnes. Alice, in one of her letters to friends,
tells of this time:

> Marjorie is one whose brain won't do its best work unless
> Brother Ass is well exercised, so my garden benefited consid-
> erably from her two month's literary labours! What fun we
> had, digging and pruning and weeding and planting – and also
> planning for the future. The local farmer who rents my lovely
> four-acre field, finishes his lease in December this year and
> Marjorie and I have all sorts of visions and plans. We are pray-
> ing earnestly that in whatever way we do use my land it may
> be 'in right ordering' as the Quakers say, that is, in line with
> the Divine Will, fitting into God's Kingdom of Righteousness
> and Love and Peace.

In 1956 there was a crisis at Rasulia, the Friends Rural Centre
at Hoshangabad in Mid-India. The two Quaker couples who had
been in charge for several years were Donald and Erica Groom and
Eric and Ruth Robertson. Donald Groom left to work with Vinoba
Bhave and Eric Robertson died suddenly after surgery for appen-
dicitis. Marjorie was asked to come to help with the reorganisation
of the work and arrived on 28th June. For the next few months she
spent two thirds of her time at Rasulia and a third at Sevagram,
where by this time there were others who could take over her responsibilities. In December she made a quick trip to England on Rasulia
business. At the end of January 1957 there was a Quaker conference at Rasulia, perhaps the most representative gathering of
Quakers thus far held in India, bringing together widely scattered

individuals and groups who had rarely or never met before. Soon afterwards new recruits for the centre arrived, and Marjorie was able to return to her full-time work at Sevagram.

There, from 1957 onwards, a new concern was developing. As Vinoba Bhave walked through Kerala he had begun to think and speak of Gandhi's conception of a *Shanti Sena*, a 'Peace Army' which might become a non-violent alternative to the police and military forces. The words 'peace' and 'army' may seem mutually contradictory, but the idea behind Shanti Sena is that those who work for peace should be as disciplined – as ready in emergencies to appoint a leader and obey orders – as any trained military force, and that only people who have that kind of discipline, both personally and as a group, can be really effective in the keeping of peace. The training is not a matter of techniques but is based on the principle that a person can be most effective in a situation of potential violence if he or she knows the local community well enough to realise what tensions are building up, so that the peace army has a dual purpose: to live among the people and serve them in whatever way is most needed, and also to be active peace 'soldiers' in an emergency.

Vinoba Bhave felt that women were more fitted than men to take the lead in this kind of 'army', and his first all-India Shanti Sena Committee consisted entirely of women, with Marjorie as convener. She and her colleagues arranged the first training camp for 'peace soldiers' at Sevagram, and some of those present went direct from the camp to deal successfully with tensions which were beginning to explode into violence in their own home areas.

Marjorie, however, had begun to be aware of some of the limitations of the large sized training groups with which she had been dealing in Sevagram and to wish that she could carry out some of the same kind of training in small, family-sized groups. There, among other things, they might learn to live and work happily with fellow students who might at first seem uncongenial, and whom in the large group it was too easy to avoid. This dream of small-scale training fitted in very well with the vision she and Alice had for the use of Alice's land.

CHAPTER EIGHT

Training Groups, Kotagiri 1959-64

IN THE AUTUMN OF 1959, Marjorie left Sevagram and made a short visit to England where she made her base with her brother in Sheffield. A special session of London Yearly Meeting of British Friends was held while she was there to consider and approve the draft of a revised Book of Discipline. Marjorie was deeply impressed by the spirit in which this was carried out, both worshipful and disciplined.

On one of her journeys between Sheffield and London she was recognised by a contemporary of hers at Cambridge, Roland W. Walls, whom she hadn't seen for 30 years. He too, she found, was leading small-scale training groups in an experiment inspired by the Bishop of Sheffield for ordained ministers preparing for work in industrial areas. The groups lived together as a family and each one was employed in some steel works or factory as an ordinary labourer, so that they gained direct experience of the problems of the families they were to serve. Marjorie was much encouraged to find something so similar in spirit to her own ideas and hopes.

When she returned to India it was to settle in Kotagiri where she and Alice began to plan in earnest. Alice's own small house overlooked a steeply sloping hillside, half of it woodland and half cultivable field, which formed an estate of about 9½ acres.

In the stimulating climate of the Nilgiri Hills vigorous work was possible. They planned that Marjorie should have her own little house built at an appropriate place on this hillside where training in non-violence and work on the land could be combined. At that time the Government of Madras State was urging Nilgiri farmers

Marjorie with her brother, Ronald, and his wife, Mary, 1959

to terrace their fields to prevent soil erosion. They offered the free service of their own engineers to plan the terracing and supervise the work, the owner of the land re-paying the cost of labour in easy instalments over a period of years. Marjorie and Alice decided to take advantage of this generous and sensible offer.

Alice describes their plan in her letters:

> It is, as you see, a really co-operative plan – I give my land, Marjorie gives her experience and her wonderful, humble spirit and equally wonderful practical good sense, the students give their labour on the land, and the Good Lord gives the inspiring beauty of these hills and lovely climate. My land, lying more or less idle and doing nobody very much good, was getting to be an awful burden on my conscience, and I am thrilled at the prospect that at last it can be used wisely and well.

After the terracing was done, the first thing to do before building a house was to find water. They hired a diviner who found water on one of the terraces half way down the hillside. Alice writes:

You can imagine the joyful excitement when they struck water. The young Bagada farmer came rushing up the hill to the house to find me: 'We've got it! We've got it! Water is coming out of a crack in the rock, and I can hear it running, ba-da, ba-da ba-da like a river, the other side of the rock'. The next day there took place a little ceremony of thanksgiving and blessing, which surely has its counterpart in Old Testament customs. I had to be out of Kotagiri that day, but Sigamani (her helper) told me about it. My workmen brought flowers and incense and a goat; they decorated the scaffolding with the flower garlands, they burnt the incense as a 'sweet savour unto the Lord', and they sacrificed the goat (poor thing!), sprinkled the ground all around the well with its blood – and then of course, built a fire and cooked and ate the flesh. I'm not Old Testament-minded, and I don't like blood-sacrifices, so I wasn't sorry to have a good alibi that day! My share in the sacrificial thanksgiving was a *small* gift of money toward the expenses; the men themselves contributed the bulk of the cost. They really *cared*. When they cut the first sod they had

Alice Barnes at her home, Ilkley

prayer too, though no 'sacrifice', except flowers and a coconut and its milk sprinkled on the spot where they were to dig. Sigamani, who is a sincere Christian, joined them, and at their request offered a prayer 'through Jesus Christ our Lord'.

The site of the well decided the site of Marjorie's future house – a few yards away along the same level terrace. The hillside was excavated and blasted to get a level site of sufficient width. A local builder was employed and set to work to build on the solid rock with the stone excavated from the site. There was enough stone not only for the house but also for a wall round the well and for steps up to Alice's house a couple of hundred feet above!

Sometimes Marjorie's ideas differed considerably from those of her builder. A window for him should be 2½ feet above the ground. 'No', said Marjorie, 'Not in this house. The people are going to sit on the floor and must be able to see out of the window from the floor. It is no good having it up there!' Windows finally were wide and low, with a wide windowsill to use as a seat.

Her little house gradually took shape – nestled in the side of the steep hill looking westward into the sunset and towards the higher ranges of hills. Alice describes it thus:

It is built of blocks of the beautiful dark grey Nilgiri granite, cut out of my hillside, and is roofed with red tiles from Kerala, and the roof timbers are from a few of my grand old eucalyptus trees (which needed felling anyway). Behind the cottage rise terrace after terrace of the field; before it descend terrace after terrace; on its right more terraces stretch away to my woods, and on its left is a bit of still wild hillside. To believe its lovely view over the valley at its feet, away up to the mountains and the glory of the sky at dawn or sunset, you must come and see it for yourselves. But only folks with stout hearts and lungs (and legs) need expect to visit it, for, in spite of the well engineered path we have made down through the woods, it's a long STEEP clamber down, and, curiously enough, a still longer, steeper clamber up again. We have had some visitors who have been content with looking down on its roof from the grass plot (lawn is too elegant a name) in front of my cottage; but it's worth the effort of going down and coming up again. After much thought and consultation, Marjorie has named the cottage 'Amaithi Aham' (all the a's are short), which is Tamil for 'Peace Homestead'. (Certain friends bawdlerised this name into 'The Mighty Atom'.)

There was no electricity, no plumbing, and cooking was over a smokeless wood stove built at table height with a chimney which created a draft and carried away the smoke. The fire reached the cooking vessels placed over holes, with a final hole next the chimney where water was heated in a big pot. It was the kind of stove that can easily be made by the villagers themselves, using their own familiar materials but eliminating the usual smoke-filled kitchen. The house had two small bedrooms, and Indian style bathroom and a larger central room with a fireplace.

Between 1960 and 1964 Marjorie gave her full attention to the training groups and the fields – except between October and mid-January – a period when cold and rain coincided. During one such period in 1960/61, Alice was hospitalised after she had a black-out the day after Christmas. Marjorie and Alice's daughter, Premila, cared for her at home until her strength returned. Alice had other physical problems that year and Marjorie was always on hand to help. Alice wrote:

> It has been a blessing to have Marjorie on hand all this year while Brother Ass has been playing his pranks with me. She has taken innumerable little burdens on her already heavily-laden shoulders. In fact she has been, and is, my very dear and faithful sister. She also exercises a sister's prerogative and scolds, or at least makes remarks when she thinks I am over-working – and gets snapped at for her pains, another sign of a true sisterly relationship!

Marjorie's plan was for groups of eight or nine people working as a community towards a deliberately non-violent way of life. She planned for units of a month each, and announced the dates and details in various periodicals which were read by people interested in Gandhi's ideas or Gandhi's form of service. Some had their expenses paid by the institutions with which they were working. Some were helped by funds available through Marjorie herself. As a good illustration, there was one particular young man who wrote and said that he would very much like to come but had no money at all. Marjorie replied that if he could manage to get himself there, she would see that the cost of the camp itself – which was very small in any case – was taken care of. He lived in the very far south – somewhere near Cape Comorin. He came – partly by walking, partly by hitch-hiking. He turned out to be a very good, serious, enterprising student. When he was about to finish the course, Marjorie had a visit from one of the senior Gandhian workers who was helping to organise social service work of various kinds in Tamil Nad. He talked with this young man and offered him a job, and he subsequently became one of the most able workers in the field.

The groups usually consisted of women and men together. It worked best when there were about five men and three women – from the point of view of how the house was built – and in all ways, it worked better to have a mixed group. There were no formal qual-ifications for entering the course – except for language. Students needed to be able to communicate in either Tamil, Hindi or English. Tamil was the local, regional language in Kotagiri; Hindi, the recog-nised all-India communication language; and English, the inter-national language. These were also among the languages that Marjorie herself could manage.

A group ideally came for a month at a time. They lived together, did all their own cooking and cleaning in the very simplest kind of camp style. They learned how to maintain very simple outside latrines in good healthy, clean condition; kept their own accounts; did daily work together in productive agriculture and had daily peri-ods of meditation. They discussed all the problems already encoun-tered in their own experience before coming and pooled ideas of the best ways of helping their own villages after they returned.

A typical group would arrive in the latter half of the morning, when the bus normally arrived from the railhead in the plains below, take baths and have lunch. Then they planned their own daily programme. They always wanted a period of worship. Marjorie herself never took the initiative in suggesting any religious obser-vance but every group raised the question and decided to have some form of morning family prayers, in spite of every group being inter-religious. Sometimes, when there were four religions among the six students, this took the form of short readings (quite often from *God of a Hundred Names*, the anthology by Barbara Greene and Victor Gollancz) and then five to 10 minutes of silence. Marjorie herself would often bring out several books of her own from which readings might appropriately be chosen. Sometimes if the group included more musically inclined people, there would be some singing or chanting – such as the Upanishadic prayer 'From darkness lead me to light'.

The group would arise about 5.30 a.m. – almost dawn – and have coffee before their period of worship. Then there would be household chores. Some would prepare breakfast; some would cut up vegetables and clean grain for later in the day. Others would clean the house and be sure the surroundings (latrines, etc.) were thoroughly clean for the day; and some would do odd jobs in the garden.

After breakfast, they would all work together doing practical garden jobs, usually one student being the leader. This involved practical training in organising as well as getting the necessary work done. This was a happy period – talking, singing, learning each other's languages – 'What's the Tamil for this? The Hindi for this?'

Then there were baths before the mid-day meal – the cooks going first, the others doing personal reading, study, or anything else as they awaited their turn. Either immediately before the mid-day meal, while the cooking was going on, or shortly after, there

Terraced hillside, Kotagiri

would be a class with fairly formal discussion. In the afternoon there would be various kinds of personal chores as people took turns going to the market, post office, getting the newspaper and bits of shopping needed – walking two miles to the village and two miles back. They would return by four o'clock. One person would write the daily diary or 'log' for the community while the others had free time. Then in the evening, before supper, there would be one more class, evening chores and the evening meal.

After supper they would sit around the fire and deal with the day's 'log'. The person who had written it would read it, and it would be discussed by the others. Very good training emerged naturally. Some of the 'logs' of the first days would be written in the first person singular and very soon one of the others would interrupt and say 'That's all about what *you* were doing, but what were *we* doing when you were doing *that*?' There were some who only reported the good things. Here is where Marjorie would come in with 'What about that mistake made when you didn't know the difference between the weed and the crop?' or 'What about the burned rice?' They could see and learn from their mistakes. Then they would do the accounts: when is it right to put a thing down

Marjorie's house

as a community expense and when is it a luxury not to be paid for by the community?

There was also opportunity for adventure and initiative in new situations. This usually took the form of Saturday excursions, each one more demanding than the former one. The first excursion was always to Ooty (the hill station, Ootacamund) because it was a famous tourist attraction and the students coming from all over India looked forward to being close to this special place and wouldn't really be satisfied until they got there. It was a good beginning for an adventure because on the way from Kotagiri to Ooty is the highest hill in the Nilgiris. They went by bus until they reached the saddle, the highest point in the road from which one could get easily to the top of the hill. When they got there, they could see the mountains round about and the general topography of the Nilgiris. Then they went down a very steep shortcut from the top of the mountain into Ooty more than a thousand feet below. On the way down, they went through vegetable gardens which inspired them all – every inch used by the local market gardener – and they saw a lot of new temperate-zone vegetables which most of them had never seen before. On one occasion as they were admiring a vegetable garden, the woman owner came up to Marjorie and thrust into her hand a little bag of new potatoes. 'I have just dug these' she said 'and I must give some of my first fruits to somebody' – a special custom of giving away part of your first harvest. They saw the botanical gardens in Ooty itself, with plants and trees from all over the world, and they experimented with rowing boats on the lake. They finally went home on the bus.

When they got home very pleased with having seen Ooty, two things happened: one was that they said 'Oh, Kotagiri is much nicer', and they were quite content to spend their time in Kotagiri. Secondly, Marjorie had them add up the number of miles they had walked that day and when they found that they had walked 11 miles without realising it, they were so pleased with themselves that they were ready to tackle anything the next week.

The next week would be an excursion which involved an outward walk of about 11 miles. It was much more difficult than the Ooty one, including a pretty good climb from which, if they wished, they could return by bus. It was a very beautiful place and this involved more than the Ooty trip because meals for the day

70

and first aid equipment had to be carried. They had to decide what might happen and what to be prepared for; how to carry things without overburdening anyone; and how to read a map and foresee when there was to be a steep climb.

The third excursion would be a similar one but further and with more steep climbing and without any alternative bus. The real test was to get to the top of a most magnificent wild hill. Between that hill and the cottage at Kotagiri was an enormous valley. This meant that they had to walk steeply down hill about 2,500 feet – up 2,500 feet on the other side and reverse the process coming home. The total distance being well over 20 miles through forest and all sorts of wild areas. This was all done in a single day – starting at early dawn and carrying breakfast as well. They would come home cheerfully with still enough spirit to bargain with market gardeners on the way for good fresh vegetables to bring home.

At the end of their particular training period, the individual students would usually return with renewed enthusiasm and inspiration to the work from which they had come – teaching jobs, especially those in teacher training colleges, or work in Gandhian institutions. One became a leading worker in the Gandhian Centre in Benares. Sometimes the experience would lead a student in a totally new direction. One young woman from Sri Lanka stayed for two terms and then did some travelling with Marjorie to various Gandhian centres. She eventually married an agriculturalist and they emigrated to Australia and then on to Papua New Guinea where her Gandhian training especially fitted the needs of the people there with whom they worked.

Alice describes:

> . . . two very interesting 'camps' of Shanti Sena (Peace Army) instructors were here; young, or not-so-young men, who are working in villages to establish centres of reconciliation, while at the same time carrying on their ordinary callings, men who are convinced that non-violence or pacifism, is a practical, constructive way of life, and that, in the words of the Shanti Sena Executive, 'the power of non-violence is not meant to secure victory in a conflict for any party, but only to establish truth and friendship'. Three weeks of living together (at very close quarters in Marjorie's little cottage), of sharing all the

household chores and fieldwork, of study and discussion with Marjorie, brought the students into very practical contact with all manner of situations in which, if we don't deliberately 'seek peace and ensue it', friction can, and will, give birth to enmity and war in varying degrees.

There were times between training groups when Marjorie was called away for peace keeping work. One of these times was in 1962 during the border trouble between India and China. She went to the North East Frontier with a small deputation of Sarvodaya workers to find out on the spot what relief or constructive jobs were needed or could be partially financed by pacifist groups. Marjorie had gone representing more especially Friends, Fellowship of Reconciliation and other Christian pacifist groups in India.

Previous to that Marjorie had been at a Friends' Advisory Committee at Rasulia where Mid-India Yearly Meeting Friends were sincerely troubled – longing to be of use to their country in this war crisis, but quite sure it was their duty to hold to the peace testimony. Many or them were being pressed by the authorities in Railway and Schools to give one month's salary to the 'defence fund', and were feeling that they must find alternative ways of sacrificial giving. Marjorie went on from that meeting to the Annual Sarvodaya gathering and her trip to the North East Frontier was the result of the two gatherings.

CHAPTER NINE

Non-Violent Groups, North America 1964

THE TRAINING GROUPS had to be stopped for awhile when in June 1964 Marjorie was chosen by the Indian Shanti Sena (Peace Army) to respond to an invitation from the North American Regional Council of the World Peace Brigade, headed by A. J. Muste and Charlie Walker. They wanted her to help in summer training camps in non-violence for peace workers in the United States and Canada. This was the result of Charlie Walker's visit to Kotagiri the previous year and his participation in one of Marjorie's training groups, as part of his study of the Indian Shanti Sena.

Marjorie arrived in New York on 17th June and stayed in North America until 22nd August. She spent the major part of her time in three main areas: the civil rights movement, chiefly in the South; the training centres for non-violent action in Connecticut; and those led by Murray Thompson of the Canadian Peace Committee at Grindstone Island, Ontario. In gatherings sponsored by Quakers, she had fruitful contacts with black thinkers and leaders as well as with many white Americans who were working for the same ends.

Marjorie was troubled by some features of the white training camps which she visited. In her own words:

> The first thing that I felt critical about, coming as I did from the Indian tradition, was the apparently almost complete lack of personal discipline on the part of these people who were supposed to be non-violent activists – shown by the sort of mess and untidiness in which they lived. This was so

73

completely different from the standards which we in India had learned from Gandhi, standards of extreme simplicity but clean and beautiful. This became one of my chief themes: 'For effective non-violent living, there is a personal discipline to be followed'. Another general trend seemed to be an emphasis on how to escape being hurt, how to avoid having the police turn hoses on you, etc. which was the exact opposite of the Gandhi tradition. These were the problems in the camps of the young whites. The blacks were very different. They had had discipline from Martin Luther King.

She went to a black training camp near Savanna, Georgia and found there a very cooperative group to work with, partly because Martin Luther King was so strongly influenced by Gandhi.

They had their own constructive discipline in a way that the white groups did not, particularly in training in song, singing 'Freedom Songs' (such as 'We Shall Overcome') with a verve and depth of feeling that was indescribably moving. This was reminiscent of the songs sung during the Freedom Movement in India.

At the training camp which she attended in Canada there were various role-playing groups. Marjorie was the only leader to keep her group constructively occupied while waiting for action. There again it was the Gandhi tradition in contrast to the American one.

In Jackson, Mississippi, Marjorie had a morning to spare and decided to test all the racial facilities and see what might happen. She was deliberately wearing Indian cloths – a Punjabi suit – and was well tanned from the Indian sun. 'So', said Marjorie: 'I marched into the public library and sat there reading the local newspapers to get a feeling for what was being felt and talked about locally. They didn't know what to do with me.' Later she left the library and found a bookshop – a 'John Birch' bookshop. (The John Birch Society was a very conservative group in the South in those days but the name meant nothing to Marjorie.) There she came upon a good Southern lady dressed in gloves and hat. 'Although she thought my costume rather strange, she began talking, asked me where I had come from and what I had seen. She said "You see, those Northerners don't really understand us. They don't understand the situation in the South at all".' Marjorie said 'Yes, I think

I can understand. I'm a southerner in my own country'. This opened the floodgates and the woman began talking freely. In the end Marjorie was able to suggest to her that there were two points of view, and to illustrate it from one or two things she had seen in the newspaper that morning. They parted good friends.

In *The Friendly Way* (a Quaker newsletter published in India) Marjorie shared some of the memories of that trip:

It was especially interesting and inspiring to meet so many who looked to wider issues and saw their own task as part of a larger whole. I will mention three of these issues which have, so it seems to me, world-wide implications.

The first is that non-violent negro civil rights workers were concerned for the rights of other minorities, such as the Indian population, as well as their own. In Canada, justice for both the Indian and the French-speaking minority was seen as an integral part of non-violence. Martin Luther King goes so far as to trace the arrogance of the white racist and his police brutalities not only to the legacy of slavery but to the largely unconfessed, unrepented, 'genocide' committed by the pioneers against the American Indian peoples, whose human rights seem still far from secure.

The second is the widespread interest in making greatly increased use of non-violent techniques by all those whose task it is to keep the peace. This is being discussed both in relation to State and national police forces and the maintenance of internal order, and also with regard to the work of UN peace-keeping forces. There is widespread recognition that the personnel of all such forces would need to be trained or retrained for work with a non-violent orientation, just as thoroughly as they are now trained in the use of their conventional weapons.

My third and last point is that there is a growing realisation that a struggle for a just and non-violent human society involves not merely *reform* (such as allowing negroes to vote and to compete on equal terms for job and homes; or in another field, securing a ban on atomic tests), but social and economic and political *revolution*. This was the thesis put forward in what seemed to me to be the most impressive speech

I heard during the whole of my trip. It was made by a distinguished Boston negro, Mr Noel Day. In his view, non-violence can only gain its ends if it is prepared to be revolutionary and not merely reformist.

After a little over two months, Marjorie headed back for India and on her way home, flew to Norway to take part in a conference on Alternatives to Violence in International Conflicts.

Marjorie with her nephew and niece, Brian and Dorothy, 1959

CHAPTER TEN

Nagaland Peace Mission 1964-67

MARJORIE NEEDED TO HURRY BACK to India to attend the half yearly meeting of the Sarva Seva Sangh, the organisation of Gandhian social workers, to be held in September in Madurai, South India. Time was running out so she didn't get off the plane at Bombay as planned but flew on to Madras and took the night train to Madurai, saving 24 hours and arriving in time to report on her visit to the non-violent training groups in North America. Jayaprakash Narayan, one of Gandhi's most distinguished followers, was also there to report on his successful Peace Mission in Nagaland, which had resulted in the cessation of hostilities between the Naga 'rebels' and the Government of India forces. 'JP' (as he was affectionately called) sought her out. 'Marjorie,' he said, 'I want you to go to Nagaland.' 'What *me*!' she replied in astonishment. 'I have only just got back to India. Nagaland is as far as it could be from the Nilgiri Hills and I know practically nothing about it.' 'But, Marjorie,' persisted JP, 'you don't realise what a strong position you have. Our government leaders know you as a pre-independence friend; they will give you the necessary permit. The Naga leaders will accept you because you are a fellow Christian, and not an Indian by birth.' 'All right', said Marjorie, 'I will give it a month's trial.' The month extended to nearly three years.

Background

It is important to understand some of the history leading up to the misunderstandings between the Indian Government and the

Naga people. The Naga Hills are a comparatively remote area of wild and heavily forested country bordering on China and Burma. The people have their own culture and are different in race, language and appearance from the Indians of the plains. The British gained control of the country about 1870 or 1880, because they wanted a communication with Burma. They were wise enough not to interfere with Naga customs and traditions except to forbid inter-tribal warfare and require disputes to be referred to British officers. There were only two of these; they had volunteered because they were anthropologists and very much interested in the people. A Christian Church had been established by American Baptist missionaries, after the country was settled.

This system of government worked very well, and consequently when the Japanese invaded Nagaland from Burma during the second world war, the Nagas were very helpful to the British forces, acting as scouts in the forests they knew so well and often rescuing British and Indian troops who had lost their way. When the Nagas began talking with the Indian soldiers, they heard of Gandhi and assumed that when India was free they, as a distinct people, would be given the right to determine their own status. This did not happen and instead of being given the measure of autonomy which they expected, they were given the lowest status, among those areas not considered fit for full autonomy. Disappointment led to a long period of non-violent non-cooperation with the Government of India, as they tried to follow Gandhi's methods. The Government, preoccupied with severe problems elsewhere, did nothing; from 1954 onwards violence broke out and 10 years of guerrilla warfare followed. Several efforts to end it came to nothing; the Nagas them-selves were anxious that a way should be found and in September 1964, by the efforts of JP and others associated with Gandhi, terms for a cease-fire were agreed upon.

Off to Nagaland

Marjorie went off to Nagaland feeling very humble and wonder-ing what she would find there. Her only previous contact with Nagas had been with a few Naga students who had been sent to Sevagram in the early 1950's (before the violence had begun) by a sensitive

Director of Education in Assam. What could she imagine herself doing to reconcile the conflict between the the two armies? What if the ceasefire broke down? How would she be received?

When she arrived, at the beginning of January 1965, she received a heart-warming welcome from the Naga Church leaders as they gathered round a seasonable fire. It brought her right into a new wealth of friendship in a fellowship of common work. JP's 'Peace Mission' had rented a house in Kohima to serve as a 'Peace Centre'. It was a welcoming, friendly place.

> One evening [wrote Marjorie], half a dozen villagers hailed us from the road, came in, examined our simple 'amenities' with astonishment and friendly laughter, clasped our hands warmly and went their way. Alas, we had no common language except smiles, so we could not find out who they were or where they came from.

Meanwhile, Nehru, India's Prime Minister, had made Nagaland into a State of the Indian Union, with Kohima as its capital. People from its mixed Naga and Indian society came to the centre to talk about special needs such as village industries, medical services, or the dearth of good school books written with Naga conditions in mind. There were overnight guests who sometimes had to spread their bed rolls all over the living room floor; at other times a member of the Peace Mission might be there alone.

When Marjorie first arrived in Nagaland, the Church leaders made her a tour programme so that she could meet people of various tribes and learn as much as possible about conditions. This was helpful, enjoyable and strenuous. The Government helped by providing a jeep, painted white, to symbolise it's peaceful mission. Sometimes 'it's innards would go on strike' at awkward times and places as they bounced over the rough forest roads. But hospitality, both in Naga villages and military outposts, was ready and generous, and she was never seriously stuck.

> Once [said Marjorie], I rode 20 miles on a Naga 'bus' – ie. a Government truck which, like everything else on wheels in Nagaland (except military convoys) takes on anyone who needs a lift. The magic words 'Peace Mission' gave me a first class seat in the cabin, and although the road was very narrow and in parts rather unstable, the Naga driver handled his vehicle

with such care and skill that one felt complete confidence. By his side stood a shot-gun, and every now and then, at a shout from the passengers behind, he would stop the truck and, with one or two cronies, disappear after game into the roadside scrub. However, rather to my relief, they returned each time empty-handed. When we reached his destination I was able to find other transport for the remaining 50 miles to Mokokchung; after a few miles, we encountered a whole herd of deer, and I felt rather glad that my friend with the shot-gun had been left behind!

Nagaland had been granted Statehood only in 1962, and although some Nagas had accepted this and entered the State government, others had by then become so embittered that they continued to fight for complete independence. It was with these 'underground' leaders that a 'cease fire' had been negotiated. The government then began to hold talks with them at a special 'Peace Camp' in a village just outside Kohima. There had already been one meeting before Marjorie arrived, and she was invited to join the second. It was soon apparent that there was no agreed record of the proceedings of the first meeting. Marjorie's first job was to act as recorder, for the language used was English.

At the next meeting both sides arrived angry, the Government accusing the 'underground' of breaking the terms of the ceasefire, and the Nagas hotly denying it. The outcome was an agreement to set up an 'Observers Team' to investigate these and future complaints whenever they occurred. By then, at Marjorie's sugges-tion, Dr Aram, a sociologist from South India, had joined the Peace Centre. He and Marjorie formed the core of the Observers Team, and a military and civilian officer from each side were appointed to work with them – six altogether. They were given a white jeep for transport and asked to get the facts of each case and report their findings to both sides, with recommendations for what should be done. This worked. At first the people had had no faith that the ceasefire would last, but with each day of continued peace they began to have more confidence.

Each day was a challenge; the Observers Team never knew what it might bring. Complaints arrived and they would have to decide which allegations needed to be investigated at once and which could be dealt with by letter or interview. Both parties had to be informed of the complaints against them, and receive copies of the investigators' reports – all of which required a great deal of correspondence.

Much time was spent in listening – active and alert listening which gets below the surface – to the feelings and attitudes of the speakers. The fact that so much had to be done through translation or in a language in which the speaker was not at ease, made the whole process very difficult. The need to pick out the elements which might enable a compromise to be reached and to present suggestions so as to produce a positive response, added to the challenge.

Suddenly a crisis came! The 'Naga National Day' was to be celebrated (by the underground) on 22nd March. In the place where it was originally planned there was a water shortage, and the venue was changed to a high spur of the hills which overlooked Kohima. This was the very spur from which the Japanese had attacked Kohima during the war. Rumours flew and multiplied – the Naga army, it was said, had re-dug the Japanese bunkers and was fortifying the hill! They were going to attack the town! The Observers climbed the spur to see for themselves, and were able to assure the Indian security forces that the Japanese bunkers were still peacefully overgrown with bushes and that no fortifications were built or planned. In Marjorie's words:

> For the next four days and nights we shuttled to and fro between Government House Kohima (interviewing the governor in his bed in the middle of the night), and the hill top camp, seeking out 'growing points' of reconciliation. Both sides behaved with great generosity; the 'underground' agreed to withdraw all their military personnel to a more distant jungle camp, and use them only at the celebration itself; the Government of India representatives agreed to make no objection to a formal military Guard of Honour for the 'underground' civilian leaders. We hoped eagerly that a full understanding might be reached, but in the end we failed to get written assurances from the 'underground' in terms acceptable to the Kohima authorities. At 3 a.m. on the 22nd we went home to bed depressed. At 6 a.m. the Government declared a curfew in Kohima which had the effect of preventing many hundreds of villagers from setting off for the celebration. Our telephone

began to ring – Naga friends describing the rising tension – would we come? More 'shuttling' between the police officers on one side and the waiting processionists on the other; more willing compromise. The procession went forward, agreeing to use tracks and short cuts only and to avoid the main road. Good humour was restored, the celebrations were held in peace and with no military display, although they were watched by sundry Indian Army units hidden in the forest above, and the road to Kohima was guarded.

There were some reports that required speedy action if 'faces' were to be saved. One such came from a village two days' journey away by road. Marjorie continues,

We sought the help of the understanding Chief Secretary: could he provide a really reliable jeep at once? 'I'll see what I can do,' he replied. A little later the telephone rang: a helicopter would be at our disposal early next morning! Within five hours we had visited the village, dealt with the potential trouble, and returned to Kohima with our report. Twenty-four hours later it might have been much more difficult for those who were breaking the truce terms to withdraw without losing face.

Sometimes amusing things happened. Soon after her arrival in Nagaland, JP told Marjorie, whose normal attire was the Punjabi women's full trousers and long top, that she had better not wear such clothes in Nagaland because Punjabis were so unpopular there. In the future Marjorie therefore wore ordinary slacks, a blouse and a jacket. One day she was standing by the jeep at the police post at the frontier of the Nagaland and Manipur States (for there were Naga populations in both and the 'ceasefire' covered both) waiting for the driver to complete formalities. She had tied a scarf over her hair to keep out the dust. Two Indian soldiers came by and as they passed one said to the other in Tamil 'Is it a man or a woman?' Marjorie shouted in Tamil after their retreating backs – 'Oh, it's a woman all right'! They swung around, their faces a picture of astonished delight, and came running back. A Tamil unit had just taken over the military checkposts all along that road, and they were so pleased to hear their native tongue that they invited Marjorie to celebrate Pongal (a South Indian January holiday) with them. From then on if the team was in a hurry and approached one of the check points, all they had to do was to lean out of the jeep and shout in Tamil and everything opened up.

Whatever success the Observers Team had – and there was a great deal of success – was largely dependent upon Gandhi's principle that you deal face to face with the people concerned, get them to meet each other whenever appropriate, talk it out, and get each side to see the other point of view. They were able to work as successfully as they did because they were known to be interested in the truth; were known to be impartial; had no axe to grind; and were telling the truth as far as they could find it out. In addition, they were obviously not armed, nor had they any kind of police protection. After three years of work of this kind, confidence had been restored.

One of the most frequent sources of friction arose from conflicting ideas about the proper administration of justice. India in general had continued the system introduced by the British with its possibility of appeal from a lower to a higher court. In Nagaland, offenders were dealt with in their own village by the village elders who in that small and intimate community had no difficulty in ascertaining the facts, and meting out the appropriate penalty without delay. When as often happened in the years of conflict, a crime was committed by an Indian against a Naga, and everyone knew what had happened, Nagas resented appeals to a distant court where the culprit might be acquitted on a mere technicality. Marjorie sometimes found herself arguing with high placed officials who maintained that it was 'impossible' for two different legal systems to operate in one country, and whom she embarrassed when she pointed out that England and Scotland had managed to stay united for centuries with different legal systems intact!

This matter of justice was just one aspect of a very live and practical tradition in which each village managed its own affairs, grew its own food, wove its own cloth in its own distinctive pattern, built its own houses and grain stores. When Marjorie met some of the men who 15 years earlier had been her students in Sevagram, one of them said to her:

> Now you see what I meant when I wrote in my final evaluation of my course there, that Gandhi's vision of a self-governing, self-reliant village was to be found realised in my own country.

The 'cease-fire' covered the whole area inhabited by the Naga peoples and that included, as has been said, the northern half of Manipur State. Manipur State was due for an election in 1967. The memories of previous elections in that area were very unhappy ones. After consulting the people in the Manipur government, Marjorie and Dr Aram tried to visit all the villages, especially in the most sensitive areas. They divided the areas between them, Dr Aram visiting some and Marjorie others. When it became too steep and too rough for any jeep to go, Marjorie and Dr Aram would walk, tramping over a very difficult terrain. In each village they tried to explain to the people what the legal requirements were. For example, they explained to them that it was required by law that the vehicle carrying the ballot box be guarded. When they saw two soldiers in the jeep with guns, it didn't mean that they were coming to attack, but that they were merely guarding the ballot box. They also explained that if villagers didn't want to vote, they didn't have to vote. In the event, villagers received the election party with courtesy, hospitably supplied their physical needs, but sometimes sent them back with an empty box!

The last village that Marjorie visited in Manipur State was one where the election ought to have been held already. The election party had set off, but had returned without reaching the village, saying it wasn't safe to go any further. The election was therefore postponed and Marjorie set off for that village the day before it was to take place. That day can be best described in Marjorie's own words:

> We set off in a jeep down one of the regular beautiful Naga roads, a narrow but very well graded path along the side of the hill which normally they walk but on which a small jeep can go. It was 15 or 16 miles. We had gone about five miles when turning a corner we found an enormous great tree down across the road. It was impossible to pass, so we said to the driver, 'you stay here, we will walk down and you wait for us to come back'. Off we went, and I soon began to understand that what had scared off the election party wasn't militant Nagas but *wild elephants;* there were many signs of elephant droppings and broken bamboos, etc. The townsmen in the jeep didn't like the look of this, so they had gone back. We went down to the village and found everything was all right.

We explained that the election party would come along if they could the next day, and we set off back again. I had just said to my companion 'I think It's only another two miles or so to where we left that jeep', when round the next corner there *was* the jeep. The driver said 'Well, after you'd gone, a party of Nagas came along and asked "What's this jeep doing here?" And I told them and they said "Oh, if we'd known the *Nagaland Mother* was coming we'd have cleared the road"'. They had set to work with their axes and cleared off the tree that blocked the road. When we got near the last village higher up, probably the village from which these men had come, there was a whole party waiting by the roadside to greet us with little presents of eggs and things. So we left Manipur very happily and came back to Kohima.

There was one occasion when the team got very angry reports from the Nagas. The soldiers in a certain camp, they said, had gone further from camp than the ceasefire terms allowed, and had killed a lot of fish in the river with explosives. Marjorie went directly to the camp commander. 'I can understand very well' she said 'that your men must be very hungry for some fresh food, getting nothing but tinned stuff as they do. But the fish supply is very important to the Nagas, and they are very careful to take only the large ones not the small ones. They let the small fish grow so there are always some more.' The commander was very responsive. He said 'We are very sorry. We didn't know that. I'll see that it doesn't happen again'. And so Marjorie went to the Naga village and said 'They are very sorry and they have promised that it won't happen again'. Marjorie told them the reason for stealing the fish was that these poor fellows were getting no fresh food at all. So the Nagas said, 'Right, we understand'. Marjorie heard afterwards that a day or two later some Nagas had turned up at the gate of the camp with a haunch of venison and said: 'We were able to kill a deer in the forest. We hear that you are very short of fresh food and so we have brought you a little'. The people in the camp were very touched and insisted on giving the Nagas a bit of sugar in return. Later on the relations in that little corner of Nagaland became so friendly that football matches were going on between the young men in the Indian army camp and the young men in the 'underground' army camp in the jungle – something which was not 'supposed' to happen!

By 1967 it was possible to leave the local civilian officers of the two parallel 'governments' of Nagaland to deal together, in a friendly spirit, with complaints affecting their own village; it was also possible for the two military members of the Observer Team to go together to settle complaints about military movements. Reluctantly Marjorie left Nagaland; there were reasons for returning to Kotagiri.

CHAPTER ELEVEN

Kotagiri Years 1967-71

MARJORIE HAD COMPELLING REASONS for returning to her home in Kotagiri. Alice Barnes, 16 years older than herself, was having a number of health problems, including failing sight, and Marjorie wanted to be there to help whenever she could. Marjorie came home to Kotagiri at the end of March 1967. During the first year after her return, she did do some travelling on Quaker or Gandhian affairs, but short trips only, so that she could be on hand when needed.

One of the first trips was to nearby Ootacamund to help with the Colloquium – 'a talking together' between Hindus and Christians of various schools of thought and practice – organised by Douglas and Dorothy Steere. Two or three Quakers resident in India helped to form a 'Quaker Core' and Marjorie was one of these Friends. The theme chosen was 'The Inward Journey' and as they all shared their own spiritual pilgrimages, they came to 'know one another in that which is eternal'.

There were occasional trips to the Gandhi Museum in Madurai, an overnight train trip, and it was here that I myself first met Marjorie – an occasion I will always remember vividly. Mutual friends had put us in touch with one another. When I came to the door of the guest house, there she was – tall, slender, grey hair pulled back in a bun, sparkling dark eyes and a radiant smile – strikingly beautiful in a simple, white, homespun Punjabi outfit. But even more, there was a force of spirit that emanated from her – a transforming spirit that I was to discover later had changed many lives as well as my own.

Rosalind Baker also recalls her first meeting with Marjorie. It was at Friends House in London in 1964:

> She was to interview me before I went out to be at Rasulia as a sort of volunteer. I'd *heard* of her, and felt awe in anticipation. My train was late. I arrived half an hour late for the interview, and was ushered into a room where a tall rather gaunt woman (wearing what I later learned was a Punjabi outfit), stood in profile (and you know Marjorie's aquiline *profile*!) looking out of the window. Then she turned, held out both hands and smiled. I began to apologise for my lateness, but she stopped me, saying, 'I want to tell you a story'. Then she told me about the Indian train which during the war years had arrived spot on time (in those days Indian trains never *did* arrive on time) and everybody wondered what had happened – until it was realised that this one was *yesterday's* train! We both laughed, and any ice there may have been between us immediately melted away. A great gift for putting people at ease!

Young people from all over the world, hearing about Marjorie through some grapevine or other, recognised this transforming power and found their way somehow to Kotagiri or wrote to her. One young Friend, Barbara Hudson (now Johnson), tells of a time when, as a recent college graduate, she came to South India on a fellowship, and having been impressed with something Marjorie had written, wrote to tell her so. A few days later Marjorie appeared on her doorstep, visited with the four young people there, subsequently stayed for supper, and later as they all sat on the floor, Indian style, talking, Marjorie, weary from her travels which were usually in simple third class train accommodation, curled up on the floor and went to sleep. Barbara said she had never felt more complimented. Marjorie describes this affliction in a letter: 'When sleep comes, it descends on me like an avalanche, to use the words of one of my friends who is similarly afflicted'. They gathered together on the roof the next morning for a Meeting for Worship, and years later Barbara remembered Marjorie's ministry that morning – spoken gently and quietly, quite in contrast to her usual vigorous speech; and felt sure that her message had come from the Source.

Barbara also describes a bus ride with Marjorie later that day – it was sunset time, in all its beauty, and 'we sat quietly without talking. I felt in awe of Marjorie, but it was a comfortable, friendly awe which made that ride memorable. It seemed right not to need to talk'.

In contrast, she remembers seeing Marjorie off at the train station and how 'she organised, in loud Tamil, the people getting in and out of a third class compartment as she was trying to get in. Truly impressive!!'

Marjorie was most content, though, working in her fields in Kotagiri enjoying the peace and beauty whatever the season. She often described her life there in letters to friends:

> I'm so glad that you feel the beauty all round; the last two mornings before breakfast I've been broadcasting buckwheat on one of the beds and digging it in; and all the while as one lifted one's head there was beauty everywhere and a blackbird simply singing his heart out.
>
> I must give your greetings to the weeds. We spent a most satisfactory hour this morning digging them out of the ex-garlic bed before sowing peas. It was just the right time when they were well grown and easy to pull and had not yet sent out their numerous progeny into the surrounding soil.

Marjorie usually arose about 5 a.m., well before dawn, and after a good cup of coffee, did her writing before it was light enough to go out into the fields:

> I really must stop; the light is now dawning and my lantern is slowly going out for lack of oil (none left in the house – bad housekeeping!!) so I must concentrate on what I can manage in a half light until it is fully day.

And at a very different time of year:

> There comes a day in December, in the Nilgiri Hills, when the Northeast Monsoon has washed the air clean; we may stand once more on the Kotagiri ridges and look away and away, across nearly a hundred miles of softly sunlit plain, to the far high ridges in the south which have been invisible for so long. New horizons emerge, beauty takes on a new dimension.

One of the joys of Kotagiri was the Quaker Trio – Alice Barnes, Mary Barr and Marjorie – referred to as 'The Three Graces', 'The

Three Witches', or even, naughtily 'The Trinity'. As Alice once described their relationship in the *Friends World Newsletter*:

> The tiny Friends' Meeting for Worship in the lovely Nilgiri Hills of South India – three resident members and an occasional, very occasional, visitor. Three of us and all quite decidedly 'diverse'! But we have had many truly gathered meetings, and when looking into one another's eyes at the end, we have known beyond any manner of doubt, and with no need for words, that we have been together in the Holy of Holies.

In June of 1968 (6th–10th June), a little over a year after Marjorie had returned from Nagaland, the little group hosted the gathering of 'Scattered Friends in India'. Marjorie, younger than Alice or Mary and full of vitality, took most of the responsibility. It was a memorable time, partly because 'those days of fellowship seemed to centre to a great degree around Alice Barnes' depth of spirit and delightful humour'. Less than two weeks later Alice had gone on to a new life, having died in her sleep early in the morning of 21st June.

In a letter to Alice's friends Marjorie wrote:

> The funeral service was held in her own beloved home. The coffin lay covered with bright Kotagiri flowers, in front of the wide windows where so many of you have sat to enjoy the loveliness outside. The gathering witnessed to the breadth and variety of her friendships: townsmen and villagers, rich and poor, Hindu, agnostic and Christian – Christians of many traditions. We were able to include in the service a time of deep silence, and one or two readings from the Quaker 'Book of Christian Discipline'. Then came the committal, in the quiet burial ground among the hills she so loved, and on a day of cool sunshine, wind and flying cloud – the kind of day in which she had always specially rejoiced.

On 8th July there was a memorial service in Madras at the Bentinck School where Alice had been Principal for so many years and the friendship between Alice and Marjorie had begun.

Marjorie's responsibilities as executor of Alice's estate helped occupy her thoughts and brought the kind of comfort that comes from being able to carry out the wishes of a dearly beloved friend. But it was a hard time for Marjorie. She wrote to a friend,

It is a merciful thing that a sudden death like this leaves one as it were a bit numb. I know that there *will* be hard times, during the coming months and years, when I shall feel very much this cutting short – on this plane – of a 40 years' comradeship. But my feeling now is that I want to do all there is to do as thoroughly and sensitively as she herself would have done. And in the meanwhile, the 'good earth' has much healing power and I make time for my fields also. I felt Alice was very near us during the service in her home.

And as time passed, Marjorie wrote:

It's a lone haul sometimes – all the *little* trivial incidents we have always shared and I therefore find myself thinking 'I must tell Alice that . . .'.

I just seem to have to go on living from day to day and hope that the pattern will gradually become clearer.

It must have been lonely sometimes in her little house.

It's a dark monsoon day – we live in a wet cloud which from time to time drops gentle rain.

Marjorie weeding her garden in Kotagiri

Can you picture me with a *fire* in the living room mid-afternoon, steady *heavy* monsoon rain outside, dark skies and a blanket of fog. . . . This is the most monsoon-like day we have had the whole season, right at the end when it *should* be finished.

There continued to be a series of sorrows and difficulties in Marjorie's life. On 4th December, the second of the Kotagiri Quaker trio, Mary Barr, died suddenly in the home of a close friend in Secunderabad where she had gone partly to escape the most severe cold in Koatagiri at that time of year and partly to visit old friends and her foster daughter.

'Chappie', Edith Chapman, my neighbour, who used to work in the Mizo District (very close to Nagaland with a very similar culture), is being *so* kind to me. She makes me go and spend the night there whenever I feel lonesome – as I *do* sometimes, now that there are *three* empty houses, where I used always to have a welcome – Alice's, Mary's and one belonging to a dear kind old lady called Elizabeth Preston who died in October.

In September of 1969, Marjorie's adopted daughter, Rani, died from cancer when she was only 36 years old, leaving behind her husband and two little girls, seven and nine. They were all part of a 'joint family' pattern – several little houses in one family compound. There were always uncles, aunts, and cousins around and at Rani's death, the grandparents immediately moved in to care for the children. As is the custom in Indian families, it is the husband's parental home to which the newly married couple goes and Marjorie had no real responsibility for the children.

Then came the sudden death of her friend, Chappie, who had drawn so close to Marjorie and been so supportive since Alice's death.

Since the time of the gathering of 'scattered Friends in India' at Kotagiri in June 1968, Friends in India, particularly Marjorie, had felt a responsibility to help a young Indian woman who had been commended to the care of Friends because of former Quaker contacts in Norway where she had originally gone for nurses' training. On her return to India, it gradually became clear that she was schizophrenic and her condition was gradually worsening. Marjorie often had her in her home – a real nervous strain – and tried in various ways to help her.

But through it all, waiting always to refresh the spirit, were the mountains round about, the birds and sunlight in the forest, and the deep silence of the starry nights.

As time went on Marjorie resumed to some extent her short courses for students in her home, but as conditions and needs changed, she found her priorities changing. She kept in touch with Gandhian friends and concerns, but gave more time to Quaker work and to the Adivasi Welfare Association work there in Kotagiri.

'Adivasi' means, literally, aboriginal, and Marjorie had been interested for some time in the work of Dr Narasimhan who was devoting his life to the service of the poverty stricken tribal people there in the Nilgiri Hills. Victoria Armstrong, an Inspectress of Schools in Britain, had visited Kotagiri to see her former teacher, Elizabeth Preston. She became so much interested in the Adivasis that she decided to devote the rest of her life to helping in whatever ways she could to support Dr Narasimhan's work. She and Marjorie became acquainted immediately, each admiring the work of the other but each also deeply involved in her own. Victoria was acting as secretary of the Adivasi Welfare Association, but when the Treasurer of the Association died, it was necessary for Victoria to take on this task. As Victoria writes:

> Now who would take my place as Secretary? No one on the Committee seemed to be willing or to have the necessary skill. We racked our brains! Then almost simultaneously Dr Narasimhan and I thought of Marjorie, but equally simultaneously the question came: 'Will she not be too busy to take on this responsibility?' But she agreed immediately – reminding us all that if you need help, it usually comes from a busy person.

From that day on Marjorie and Victoria worked closely together. Victoria continues,

> It soon emerged that Marjorie knew much more about accounts and bookkeeping than I, and I owe the foundation of my present knowledge to her. So in practice, as Treasurer, I only signed and drew cheques and continued with my general secretarial duties.

Marjorie digging in her garden in Kotagiri

Marjorie and Victoria formed a good team. They often informally switched tasks.

Alice Barnes and Mary Barr had been co-editors of the *Friendly Way* (then described as a quarterly newsletter about the thoughts and activities of Friends and their associates in India and Pakistan). When they died, Marjorie became editor. The little magazine expanded to include 'Friends in Southern Asia', and then finally became 'A Journal of Quaker Thought and Action in Asia and West Pacific Countries'.

This 'labour of love' included much Friendly correspondence which drew Friends together the world over. Marjorie's thoughtful editorials and the organising of the news she received into themes which expressed and answered the concerned of Friends, occupied her in her little 'Friendly Way office' at home and during her many train trips.

During Marjorie's journeys she occupied herself writing, editing, translating and often sewing. Friends all over the world remember Marjorie's habit of relaxing or easing tension by tearing apart one garment (usually one given to her by a friend) and creating another, sewing by hand in small, neat stitches. After a series of problems that made her train 10 hours late getting into Bombay, she wrote:

> I employed my enforced 2nd day on the train, and endeavoured to ignore the heat and dust, by working off my aggressive – destructive energies on your dark blue-cum-grey striped frock! I wonder if you'll know it? Removed that hot, lined collar, and the flap at the back of the neck, and the bottom half of the heavy sleeves, and the heavy facings of the front opening. Cut strips from the last named to bind the shorter sleeves, used the 'flap' to make flat facings for a square neck, made a pocket out of one side of the collar, and used the surplus sleeves and the rest of the collar to insert pleats at each side of the skirt to make it wide enough for free walking. I still have to restitch the hem and put on the pocket and the buttons; the overall effect is decidedly less 'professional' but from my point of view much more comfortably *wearable*, so I can *wear* it and remember you!

Marjorie's travels over the years often took her to Rasulia where she was a member of the Governing Board. Patricia Hewitt, for many years the clinic nurse there reminisces in *The Australian Friend* (July 1975):

> We always knew when Marjorie had arrived. By looking from our back verandah up at the Guest House clothesline we could see a pair of Punjabi trousers stretched out their full width (four feet!) to dry! Marjorie without a doubt! The Punjabi type kurta (shirt), duputta (scarf) and pyjama (trousers) was what we saw Marjorie in most of the time. They were always made from Khadi cloth, the hand spun, woven and printed cotton worn by all Gandhians in India. Her clothes were hand stitched and were plain, simple, and practical, especially for travelling.
>
> When the Guest House was occupied by other visitors, Marjorie stayed in our home and had most meals with us. In my early days of first meeting her, I must confess I was a little overawed by her strength of character, especially after I heard she had played Scrabble (our daily habit) with Shri Radhakrishnan, a past President of India!
>
> Marjorie always rose from bed soon after 5 a.m. and had done about two hours work before we had risen! But she never made us feel we should do likewise. My feeling of being over-awed by her presence has changed. I feel now she is a real friend for whom I have great respect. Marjorie's sense of humour, her wisdom and common sense, her gentleness and sensitivity, are the reasons why all hold her in such respect and love.

Rosalind Baker, at Rasulia during this same period, also remembers Marjorie's arrivals there from time to time en route from Nagaland to her home in the Nilgiri Hills. Rosalind was impressed with Marjorie's wisdom and

> special gift for intermediary peacemaking, spiced with good blunt Yorkshire outspokenness and common sense, and a great sense of humour. But of course, the first thing that comes to mind is her radiant smile which lights up her rather austere countenance.

Children also were impressed and influenced by Marjorie. Maggie (Margaret) Stein Squire recalls:

In 1962 when I was eight years old I went, with my parents, brother and sisters, to India. We went to live in Rasulia, the Quaker Rural Centre right in the middle of India – a tiny, busy place where many, many unusual and interesting people would come and go from many parts of the world. Marjorie came, for she was on the Board of Directors. Marjorie was the most extraordinary of all the people who visited, in the eyes of us children. She was not a comfortable, cuddly person. She was gaunt and handsome of features. I thought she had a beautiful face but the beauty of a rugged mountain and the eyes of an eagle. We watched her from the hidden view of childhood. She was very tall, she always wore very baggy Punjabi clothes, they were made of hand woven rough cotton usually in pale colours – huge baggy trousers, long plain top coming down to her knees and a piece of cloth which hung over her shoulders and drooped down behind.

Agnes Stein and Marjorie Sykes in front of Marjorie's house in Kotagiri,
1964

97

We heard wonderful stories (never directly from Marjorie and we never had the courage to ask such a mysterious person). But we had heard of her climbing mountains with sides so steep most people would be daunted; to visiting isolated tribes on the border of India who were 'head hunters'! I don't know the facts of these stories, I just recall what we as children gleaned from various people. We knew she had known Gandhi and had been friends with him so she must be important!

For a short period I and my brother were sent to boarding schools in South India and whilst there our mother and two younger sisters came during a half term for a short holiday. That was when the wonders of Marjorie's house were revealed to us. She wasn't there at the time but we stayed in it and it was a child's dream. It was very basic and was probably very hard work for my mother trying to feed us, but I think she enjoyed it as well. Marjorie's home was on the side of a steep mountain in South India in the Nilgiri Hills (known as the Blue Hills). There were hundreds of steps, steps that had just been cut out of the earth. There were many Eucalyptus trees and being up in the hills it was often misty and fairly cold, with the strange smell from the Eucalyptus tree resin. We could hardly contain our excitement at going down and would take short cuts by sliding down stretches of bare earth. At the end of the steps, half way down this bit of the mountain, was this place that looked like a shepherd's very simple hut made from stone. This was where Marjorie lived when she wasn't on a journey. It had no running water; all the water came from a hand pump. There was no electricity, so we used a lamp, once it got dark. I actually cannot remember much about the inside of the small house. I just remember there was very little in it. It had a deep sense of peace and I thought it was wonderful.

I left India when I was 12 years old. I have not seen Marjorie since, although I know she occasionally has visited my parents over the years. I carry her within, as an extremely important influence on me as a person. Because of her I know I as a woman can be strong in myself. I can, if I choose to, do what I feel to be important even if it is not quite as most people would do. That is a very precious gift which I received as a child from Marjorie even if she was unaware of giving it to me!

One of those visits to Rasulia in the early seventies however was a sad occasion. Some days earlier Donald Groom, who was then working for Friends in Australia, passed through India on his way from UK and during his time there visited his old family 'home'. As he had an air ticket, he decided he should not 'waste' it, and when he left Rasulia, Pat Hewitt drove him the 50 odd miles to Bhopal to take the plane for Delhi. She had hardly returned when the news came through that the plane had crashed on approach to Delhi killing all on board. Donald's ashes were sent to Rasulia and Marjorie was present when they were quietly and solemnly immersed in the lovely Narmada River.

When Marjorie wasn't travelling herself, she was often receiving visitors in her home or meeting them at train stations – young and old from all over the world. Jane Serraillier Grossfield, then a young recent Cambridge graduate, teaching in Madras, describes her visit:

> At Marjorie's house I was chiefly struck by the length of the walk downhill to it; the arrangements for getting water from the well and then heating it on a fire if one wanted a warm wash; the orange peel saved in containers outside the windows which were then candied into some kind of snack; the re-use of everything – I was checked from chucking an envelope into the waste paper bin. It was very cold, the fire was very warming and the hot porridge she served for breakfast very delicious. It was also very silent and I felt very alive and excited and close to natural rhythm in a way I was not in the city.

Another visitor wrote:

> I am more and more impressed with the spiritual force that emanates from Marjorie. There is something about her – some rare quality which is very hard to put into words. It was a real adventure of the spirit to visit her. She is a forceful, dynamic, gifted person – so perceptive of little things about you that you wonder if she is reading your mind.

Another response to a visit with Marjorie in her home:

> Her daily life is a very disciplined one and she draws you into it simply and lovingly and you soon feel more orderly inside and perhaps cleansed in some way. No one is forcing you to be that way – it just evolves naturally out of the atmosphere.

I didn't feel as if discipline was being imposed on me but more that her self-discipline was catching, as it were.

Often people's first memory of Marjorie was one of special compassion. Rosalind Baker recalls arriving at Marjorie's home feeling very unwell for several days:

> When I began to take an interest in food, Marjorie produced a mixture of vegetables, etc., but I'm afraid I didn't feel I could face it. Asked what I *did* feel I could face, in my weakness I almost sobbed, 'meat'. And dear Marjorie, *the strict vegetarian*, strode off the two miles or so to the nearest shop, and came back in triumph with a ring of sausages and a couple of cubes of chicken soup! That memory, of her caring for me, has remained with me for over 20 years.

Another friend, Margaret Morton, remembers:

> Marjorie had agreed to meet me at Trichy airport. When I emerged from customs, this tall, sprightly, grey-haired woman came forward, taking my hand in her firm grip. She was accompanied by an Indian man dressed in white. 'This is George', she said, 'and he has just been released from prison and is in need of a meal.' She sought out a taxi, giving short shrift to the touts, who were taken aback by her command of Tamil. We went to some eating place and I don't recall what we had to eat, but she made sure that George was well fed before she parted company with him.

A young Indian man making his first trip out of his home in South India to New Dehli became very ill on the train. As he lay there feeling lonely and rather frightened, Marjorie, also travelling to Delhi, appeared, took his pulse and temperature, found pure water for him to drink and cared for him all the way to Dehli – three days and two nights. He, now an internationally known Gandhi leader, looks back on this trip with gratitude and as he says, 'We have been friends ever since'.

Sometimes these memories were quite different. Another friend reminisced on her first meeting with Marjorie:

> I had heard of Marjorie through Quaker circles and when I arranged to meet her and stay for a few days at her home in the Nilgiri Hills of South India, I was vaguely expecting some saintly figure. What a shock then when she met me at the

station and we were approached by some boys who were begging and she sent them packing, loudly and in no uncertain terms, she really shouted at them, while I had been vaguely thinking I should give them something. She said they were perfectly well fed and I got the general idea that it was just because I looked like a tourist that they approached.

Several friends had their first impression of Marjorie coloured by her lashing out verbally at a small boy on the train, something which turned out to have been unjust, and she herself was ashamed and troubled by it. This tendency to lash out with impatience manifested itself from time to time. She could react strongly to anything from coffee not served hot enough to a sometimes quite innocent inaccuracy in the use of words by someone in an audience to whom she was speaking. And yet how very understanding she could be with other mistakes not so much connected with truth or accuracy. Some saw her as severe and austere, on the one hand, but with a special gentleness and tenderness, on the other. Perhaps all of this can be best summed up by the friend of many years who spoke of her '*uncompromising* but *loving* authority'.

CHAPTER TWELVE

C. F. Andrews Centenary 1971-74

CHARLES FREER ANDREWS was born on the 12th of February, 1871. His Centenary Year, 1971, was a very important one for India and for Marjorie, his biographer. The biography, *Charles Freer Andrews*, originally published in Great Britain in 1949, was reprinted in India in October 1971. Throughout that year there were many special events relating to the centenary, and Marjorie was frequently in New Delhi. Much of her time there was spent in editing a new book, *C. F. Andrews: Representative Writings,* and in research relating to it.

One event remembered by many Friends was held at Quaker House in New Dehli. Horace Alexander, who had been invited by the Indian Government to take part in the Celebration, was to speak that particular night on 'The Religious Development of C. F. Andrews'. He became ill and at the last minute, Marjorie was asked to give the talk in his place. Something very special happened that night. Marjorie was clearly being 'spoken through' and there were many moist eyes at the close of her talk. In responding to a friend who had expressed special appreciation for her message that night, she wrote:

> What you say about that CFA meeting at Quaker House confirms my own feeling that some of the time I was myste-riously being 'spoken through', as happens in a meeting for Worship that is 'in the Life'. I had certainly tried to come to that meeting 'with heart and mind prepared', seeing that Horace couldn't function – and afterwards I had little idea what I had actually said. I *did* have notes but there was some-thing that took over the shaping of the talk regardless of the

Marjorie with Martha Dart in New Delhi 1972

notes. And I am deeply grateful that this was channelled to
your needs. But I still feel it is somehow out of place to 'thank'
the one who at such times becomes the channel – we need
together to thank that Great Life in which we have moved.

Those who knew Marjorie well, and there were many of us, sensed
that at some 'deeper level', not intended or realised by Marjorie,
she was describing herself, as she described Charlie Andrews: the
capacity for friendship; the radiance; the sensitivity to beauty; how
both turned for strength and peace of heart to the beauty of nature
– the colours of the dawn and sunset, and the starlit sky of a clear
Indian night.

In November of that same year, Marjorie gave a paper at the
Andrews Seminar in which Horace Alexander also took part. Her
talk was on 'Andrews and the Religious Life of India'. In December,
her article '"Deenabandhu" Andrews – Rebel and Saint' appeared
in the *Indian and Foreign Review*. On 12th February, 1972, Andrew's
birthday, the closing celebration of the Centenary Year was held at
St. Stephens College where Marjorie delivered the Andrews
Memorial Lecture, "C. F. Andrews: The Unfinished Revolution".

Marjorie chose to use that time to consider the meaning and value of Andrews' work for us today. She started by pointing out that

> no matter how deeply Andrews was moved, he was never content with relief measures alone; he set himself to a disciplined and patient study of the real nature of the evil, penetrating below symptoms to underlying causes, and offering fundamental remedies.

She continued by quoting the words of Horace Alexander at the previously mentioned Centenary Seminar in November. 'This gentle Christian saint was the most radical social revolutionary of our century, and we still need his voice.' And Marjorie ended:

> So long as men are exploited, bullied and condemned to such abject poverty as millions are today the work of Andrews the radical revolutionary must go on. Those who would carry it forward must be armed, as he was, with deep compassion, with a clear-sighted mastery of facts, with great patience and persistence, humility and charity. Such qualities, Andrews would remind us, are the fruits of the spirit; his own burning love of humanity was a religious experience and this religion was no sentimental fantasy, far less an opiate. It was the strongest revolutionary force on earth.

Richard Cooper, Marjorie Sykes, Martha Dart and Edith Cooper in New Dehli 1972

Marjorie continued her work on *C. F. Andrews: Representative Writings* and in April of 1973 it was published. Harold Fassnidge who was living in New Dehli at the time reviewed the book in *The Friend* of 6th July, 1973:

> I was left in no doubt about what Charles Freer Andrews meant to the generation who knew him. Andrews' infinite love of humanity found, as it chanced, greatest expression in his concern for the people of India; this Christlike compassion and concern are manifest in writings which spanned the years from his first arrival in Bombay in 1904 to his death in Calcutta in 1940. I have been enthralled by our Friend Marjorie Sykes' scholarly distillation of the works of this remarkable man; this ordained priest of the Church of England who cherished the inner light; whose universal humanity reached so far beyond mere Christian dogma; . . . this most trusted English friend of three of the greatest Indians of his generation, Gandhi, Nehru and Rabindranath Tagore.

The formal Releasing Ceremony of the book is described by a friend who was there:

> It was a lovely ceremony in one of the conference rooms at the Ministry of Education. There were Gandhians there in white khadi, two or three members of the Cambridge Brotherhood in long white robes, some colourful saris, and regular bush shirts and trousers. Marjorie herself looked stunning in white khadi Punjabi attire. It was almost a glistening white and she was really breathtakingly lovely. All of a sudden everyone rose, and in came the Minister of Education in white kurta and dhoti.
>
> First of all, the chairman of the National Book Trust gave an opening talk; Marjorie was asked to say a few words which she did simply and beautifully; and then the Minister of Education gave a brief talk. Both he and the first speaker pointed out the special similarity between C. F. Andrews and Marjorie which was felt so strongly at the time of her talk at Quaker House on the Religious Development of Andrews. The Minister of Education 'released' the book by untying a package in which were two books – one hard cover and one paperback. Everyone then received a book and Marjorie was kept busy autographing while we all had tea.

Back at Kotagiri Marjorie had moved into Alice Barnes' house, Ilkley, named for the Yorkshire village where the couple who built the house had been married. Alice too knew and loved Ilkley, so she had kept the name. It stood at the top of the hill above Marjorie's own little house, which she rented out. This was partly because Ilkely needed to be occupied and partly because the walk up and down the steep hillside was becoming increasingly difficult for Marjorie due to a painful arthritic hip.

Marjorie had been asked to deliver a paper at the Friends' World Committee for Consultation Conference in Australia and spent much of that summer of 1973 preparing it. In the end she was not able to go to Australia in person, although she sent her paper which was read and discussed there. However, as it turned out, an even more exciting opportunity was to come.

Marjorie at Dehra Dun, April 1973

CHAPTER THIRTEEN

Friend from the Orient 1974-75

IN 1974 MARJORIE WAS INVITED by the Friend-in-the Orient Committee of Pacific and North Pacific Yearly Meetings (USA) to be their 'Friend *from* the Orient' for the coming year. Marjorie believed strongly in the value of an interchange of experience among Asian Friends and tried to make the *Friendly Way* a vehicle of communication, so she welcomed this opportunity. She wrote of this experience and what led up to it in a letter she sent in June 1975 to her friends:

Dear friends everywhere,

This dreamed-of Friendly journey became possible in 1974-75. Quakers in the Pacific and North Pacific Meetings of USA desire to maintain and increase their understanding of Asia, and their Friend-in-the-Orient Committee invited me to visit the area – the States of Washington, Oregon and California. Canadian Friends encouraged me to add a few days in British Columbia, and Quakers in Australia and New Zealand asked me to include them in a 'Pacific Rim' round trip. They warmly agreed to visits in Asia also, so I was able to spend a few days each in Thailand, S. Vietnam, Hong Kong, S. Korea and Japan on the outward journey, Indonesia and Singapore on the way back. There was, alas, a communications gap and the Philippines got left out. Fiji, however, got put in.

It is not easy to describe the inner quality of these experiences. I had never travelled like this before, the whole area was completely new to me; and yet after the first plunge into the unknown, leaving Calcutta for Bangkok, there was no sense of strangeness, rather a growing sureness of our basic human kinship amid fascinating diversity. It was so easy to relate to *people*, in spite of all the superficial barriers of language and circumstance – from Thai students to the Spanish-speaking Chicanos of California to the 'traditional' Aborigines of the Australian central desert.

If there is one thing more than another which made me feel that this journey was, as Quakers say, 'in right ordering', it was to find almost unlimited opportunities for pooling Indian insights into the criteria of a humane society, including those of Tagore and Gandhi, with the insights of concerned Western thinkers. Many men and women, of all ages, in families and communities, are bravely carrying on their own modest 'experiments with truth'. Many of these experiments are

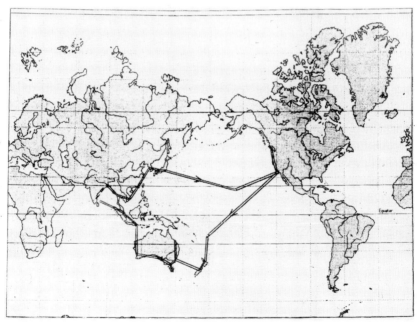

Map of the World showing Marjorie's trip around the Pacific Rim as Friend-from-the-Orient: Calcutta – Bangkok – Saigon – Hong Kong – Seoul – Tokyo – Hawaii – West Coast of North America – Fiji – New Zealand – Australia (including Tasmania) – Bali – Singapore – back to India

concerned with a voluntary limitation of our demands on the earth's resources.

Marjorie left India from Calcutta in early December and went first to Bangkok.

Bangkok

Sulak Sivaraksa met Marjorie and took her to meet with two dozen students of his study group who kept her for over three hours with good questions based on their own experience, about non-violence and its relevance. 'At the end of the three hours we paused for a meal and then went at it again!'

Vietnam

In Saigon Marjorie went to the Van Hahn Buddhist University where she met Cotri Hai, the translator of Gandhi's *Autobiography* into Vietnamese and discussed books of special interest for the University Library. She then flew north to Quang Ngai to visit the American Friends Service Committee Centre. The staff were engaged in physiotherapy and in making and fitting prosthetics for Vietnamese civilians who had been injured during the war. She appreciated the fine work being done and the very happy feel among both patients and staff. There was also a happy, simple home in which the workers and some disabled children could live.

As Marjorie travelled she found many mutual concerns – starting with that for the environment, as she visited with the Venerable Thich Tri Quang, leader of the Buddhist non-violent 'third force' which had for years 'pleaded with the contestants by word and selfless action, to stop the violence in the name of humanity'. The day before her visit with him she had been flying from Quang Ngai to Saigon over tropical forests. She looked for the scars of war and saw none; the forests had healed themselves. But when the plane came close to the southern end of the ranges, she saw hillsides laid bare by wholesale felling. She ventured to ask Thich Tri Quang if her impressions were accurate. He, Marjorie wrote, 'responded with unexpected warmth of emphasis. "No", he said, "you are not mistaken. The wealth of Vietnam is being destroyed far more rapidly today by commercial greed than by all the long years of war"'. As Marjorie continued her travels she found that the underlying concerns were the same all over the world; such as 'the truth of man's relationship to his fellow-men, the truth of his relationship to the earth which sustains him'.

Hong Kong

In Hong Kong Marjorie found a special interest in education and was asked to tape an interview with Dennis Rogers of Union Church chiefly about Tagore's and Gandhi's educational experiments. This was later broadcast on the programme 'Crossroads' and its implications for Hong Kong were the subject of discussion later. (But what Marjorie remembers is the wonderful Chinese vegetarian food served in the restaurant to which one of her new friends took her!)

South Korea

In South Korea Marjorie met Ham Sok Hon, known as the 'Gandhi of Korea', and went with him to one of the weekly meetings where Christians prayed for and remembered the political prisoners. She gave a talk later at the Friends Meeting House about her small group training classes, basic education and Indian philosophy – subjects which continued to be of interest to groups throughout her trip. She still remembers the reverent affection shown everywhere to Ham Sok Hon – especially when he saw her off at the airport. So many of the staff had been his students.

Japan

In Japan Marjorie went first to Tokyo. There at Women's Christian College she met with five groups of students, answering questions about India, Christmas at Sevagram and her nursery school in Madras. Later she spoke at the Friends Girls School to the school assembly, emphasising the difference between poverty and simplicity.

Special personal memories were: being taken to a Gagaku Society's concert of ancient Japanese music and dance – a fascinating experience; travelling to Kyoto 'by a wonderful train where even the railway tickets were works of art'; and the Japanese moss gardens there 'so simple and beautiful'.

United States

Marjorie's entrance into the United States was in Honolulu, Hawaii. She remembers the contrast between a cold winter in Tokyo (strongly reminiscent of a winter in London) and the tropical Honolulu after an overnight flight, the kindness of the taxi driver, and the lovely welcome at the simple Friends Centre there.

Marjorie's experiences in the United States were of great contrasts: her concern for the 'too much of everything – overfed atmosphere' of the culture itself – the urban sprawl with the multi-national corporations destroying ecosystems and human communities. And yet the overwhelmingly appreciative response she received from Friends and others who heard her messages. As someone said, 'Hers is a message "whose time has come" in the United States and people have been longing for what she has to give'. The truth of this statement was shown in the letters of appreciation which came to the Friend-in-the-Orient Committee after she had left. For example:

We won't know the results of her speaking and her presence at once but we can count on it.

Her classes were on fire.

She was a real channel for the Spirit to speak through and something out beyond her often took over and worked through her.

Ecology, simplicity, self-discipline – the real impact of her visit was in the area of the spirit.

Marjorie's own life style was an inspiration and provided clues to the solution to some of our most pressing environmental as well as spiritual problems.

People in those homes in which she stayed couldn't help but observe her own quietly lived disciplines.

Some of the specific examples of how individuals were affected were described in an article in the *Friends Journal* of 15th December, 1975.

Recently I saw a Friend who just a few months earlier had been overweight and unhappy. There she was – slender, vibrant, a new sparkle in her eyes. 'What happened?' I asked. 'Well,' she said, 'I was angry because I had lost respect for myself. Then I met Marjorie Sykes. Something about her took hold of me. Clearly she is an unusually well-disciplined person and I decided that's how I wanted to be. This is the result.'

A young man faced with more than he could work into each day pondered Marjorie's prescription (and example) of focusing on what needed doing and 'doing the needful' about it – which in his case meant rising an hour and half earlier in the morning. As he shared with us the joy of those quiet early morning hours when the rest of the household slept, he, too, showed a new vibrancy and sparkle.

The most important aspect of Marjorie Sykes, however is not what she has done, her experiences in a remarkable era of Indian history, or even the words she uses – penetrating and challenging as they are – but the force of Spirit that comes through her. One Friend said: 'You know, it's hard to understand – but although I remember her talk as being challenging, I don't really remember what she said because what she was – the spirit that emanated from her – was so powerful, it took precedence over everything else'.

Simplicity and self-discipline were the areas in her talks to which Friends in the United States felt most closely drawn – and not just Friends but many college students of all religious persuasions or none. The following excerpts from Marjorie's talk at a Simple Living Conference give a feeling for her message:

The call to simple living fits right into the whole question of the desperate needs and suffering in so many areas of the world. It is only as we learn how to be real stewards of our share of the universe's riches that we can help toward preserving the wealth of the world for all of its inhabitants. Our first

112

responsibility is the right *use* of the world's resources, rather than the right *sharing* of them.

We need to commit ourselves to searching how to rediscover the real values of life. In so doing we rediscover simplicity for ourselves, simple joys for ourselves, and at the same time open the way for a better life for the whole world. This means a real kind of personal discipline. When you have a focus, when you have any clear purpose, you must, if you are serious about it, select those practices which will lead to the purpose being fulfilled. The real meaning of the word discipline is to select appropriate methods to reach a chosen goal. Discipline can be a very positive and joyful thing. This is one of the many secrets of Mahatma Gandhi. He really chose for himself a disciplined life. He just quietly made up his mind 'If I am to do this job on which I'm focussed, then I must preserve my body in vigour, my mind in vigour, my spirit in serenity'. And all that is popularly called his asceticism – the wrong word, his personal discipline – the positive word, was directed to that focus. And he was one of the happiest men, one of the greatest enjoyers of life, that I have ever known.

Fiji

Marjorie left the United States on the 7th March, 1975 for Fiji. Fiji had a particular meaning for Marjorie since it was there that C. F. Andrews had made the investigations which ended indentured labour – not only in Fiji but, as a result, all over the world.

After arriving in Nandi, she welcomed the drive to Lantaka along 12 miles of deserted county lane (the *main* road around the island) – quite a contrast to the Los Angeles freeway! – the climate 'definitely Madras/Kerala – warm, green and moist, and she felt at home'.

Marjorie was particularly interested in seeing the Andrews School at Sambeto. This was the school Andrews discovered where one or two indentured Indians were trying to teach a few children under a tree. He helped to get a regular school started and, by this time, it had about 1,000 children in primary and high school sections.

As usual on this journey, local newspapers and radio stations were interested in Marjorie and she was met by a journalist for the *Fiji Sun* and had an interview with Radio Fiji. At a Mayoral reception she was given the Fijian 'welcome' beer (a root beer from ginger) served in a half coconut shell. The polite thing is to drink it straight off and then the offerer claps twice semi-bowing. Marjorie was reminded of the Naga use of rice beer on ceremonial occasions.

Marjorie was troubled to find that Fijian language and culture was not being encouraged – there was almost a 'cultural imperialism' of Indians. She passed on her concern to the Fiji-born Indian High Commissioner, who was very sympathetic. She also arranged with the External Affairs Ministry to have 12 copies of *C. F. Andrews: Representative Writings* sent to Fiji by diplomatic pouch to be distributed to libraries and suitable schools, thereby keeping alive the influence of Andrews for present and future generations.

New Zealand

Marjorie flew from Fiji to New Zealand on 12th March and landed in Aukland. She was met by Kath Knight and taken to the Friends centre. On the way she saw a road sign with an arrow 'Mt Eden Summit' and next morning as soon as it was light she set out to find that summit – only a 10 minute walk from the Centre – 'So naturally *up* I went, partly on the motor road, partly on lovely, springy turf, with oak trees here and there, and at the top, a magnificent view all round, and a very efficient guide plaque to tell you where you were looking . . . altogether very satisfactory!' But when she returned to the Centre and looked at her face in the mirror for the first time that morning, she saw her face covered with red spots 'my large nose having specially large decorations!! Was it Dengue Fever?' There had been a serious epidemic in Fiji, and she went to the doctor. He confirmed her suspicion, gave her appropriate medication and she recovered quickly. The fever is carried by mosquitoes and it is not contagious. She had a talk to give that evening on 'Simpler Life Styles and Peace', but felt that either her fever or the antibiotics kept her from being as effective as she wished. Auckland Friends thought otherwise and reported in the April New

Zealand Friends Newsletter that they 'felt blessed by her saintly presence and wisdom – and we won't soon forget those big, penetrating eyes; a school teacher it would be hard to lie to!'

In Christ Church, she had a pleasant surprise in meeting C. F. Andrews' niece (daughter of his sister, Margaret), and a great niece. What a joy to share her experiences in Fiji with them. In Dunedin, she was delighted to find John and Erica Linton, good friends, also sharing India experiences with New Zealand Friends.

Margaret West, in 'A Letter from New Zealand' in *The Australian Friend* of May 1975 wrote:

> We in New Zealand are at present enjoying the stimulation of the visit of Marjorie Sykes. She has set straight our picture of India, which had been pushed out of focus by the relief agency propagandists. We see that there are self-reliant people there, and responsible individuals who are able to support themselves. Government to government aid can involve repression rather than relief; relief societies with large funds may do very little that is really effective; the only acceptable aid is that given in personal service.
>
> Lately we have taken to saying 'It's trade not aid, that is needed'. Marjorie Sykes showed us that trade can make a bad situation worse, instancing the export of groundnuts when those who had grown them were left hungry.

As always, her talks were preceded and followed by interviews with newspaper journalists and photographers and her message clearly reached a wide audience.

Australia

Marjorie went on to Australia, as the first Fellow of the Donald Groom Fellowship. Both Marjorie and Donald Groom had worked untiringly for the Gandhi Movement in India. Marjorie was also Chairman of the Governing Board of the Friends Rural Centre at Rasulia when Donald and Erica Groom were Directors.

She flew from Christchurch on the morning of 26th March. her fellow passengers on the plane were reading the Christchurch newspapers, which contained an account, with a photograph, of her meeting of the previous day. Someone soon identified her, and she had to autograph a number of copies of that paper.

At Sydney she was met by John Fallding, who had attended the World Pacifist Meeting in India in 1949, and was taken home to his wife Vreni. So began over seven weeks in Australia – Sydney, Brisbane, Canberra, Melbourne, Adelaide, Perth.

Marjorie was delighted to find that the Fallding's home was at the end of a 'no exit' side road with a sign saying 'Track through bush reserve'. True to form she headed off into the bush whenever opportunity arose. She found that this particular area belonged to the Buddhist-Theosophist writer, Marie Byles, whom she had met (and helped nurse) about 1953 in Sevagram.

This was typical of the links Marjorie found with her past during this journey. There was, of course, Erica Groom and her daughter, Helen Groom Allan, whom she hadn't seen since Helen was a little girl at Rasulia, and Pat Hewitt who had been the clinic nurse at Rasulia. She found that the Falldings had known Camilla Wedgewood who had been at Newnham College, Cambridge with her. Camilla, though no longer living, had made her mark both as a great historian and as a warm, alive, beloved person. 'It was good' wrote Marjorie in her journal, 'to have a link with someone I had liked and admired so much as a fellow student.'

Going north to Brisbane Marjorie was met at the railway station and taken off by her young hostess for a picnic in the rain forest – so reminiscent in its luxuriance of the forests of South India. She was particularly intrigued by the 'strangling fig'. A seed planted by a bird in a crevice high up a tree trunk, sends it roots down, and its shoots up until they completely surround the host tree and kill it. The host tree rots away and the fig, a fantastically interwoven funnel, stands alone. One could stand inside, where the host tree had once been and look right up the 'chimney'. The slanting afternoon sunlight brought a golden glow into the depth through the window in the fig's root system like light falling through the windows of a cathedral.

Later on in a meeting for worship in Melbourne she had a sudden new vision of this phenomenon.

It came 'out of nowhere' [Marjorie confided in her journal], and it did seem to be a 'given', so I want to write it down:

116

The lovely forest, vibrant with life, especially the great shafts of the giants 'rooted and grounded', rising straight to the crown, with the festooned lineas and the ferns and orchids, their support. Then high up on one of these giants, a seed sown from above, by a bird, finding its crevice, germinating, growing, roots exploring downward to the soil, branches rising to mingle with and overshadow the ancient crown. And so over the years, the new tree grows by the life and strength of the old one, until at last the 'old self' crumbles away, and one may stand within the shaft, and looking upward see the lineaments of the old form preserved by the new all-embracing life and now transformed to a new beauty, illumined within by the light of Heaven. And yet both trees, the 'earthly self' tree and that which sprang from the 'Seed' from above, nourished by the same life of the earth, the same light of the sun.

Marjorie didn't consciously remember, when she tried to express this vision, that the previous Australia Yearly Meeting had been held on the edge of just such a rain forest, but it was clear that it spoke to people who had been there.

The talks she gave throughout her travels were varied:

Simplicity in the Search for a Just Society; Simplicity as Reverence for our Living Environment; The Blending of East and West; Cross-Fertilisation of Quaker and Indian Thought; New Life Styles in the Search for Peace; Tagore and Gandhi – Their Relevance Today; Basic Education and its Relationship with Social Ideals; Readings from Indian Religious Literature; Motivation for Simpler Life Styles.

Good questions were asked such as 'How do you overcome greed?'

All along, Marjorie was interested in whatever she could learn about the Aborigines of Australia because of her own work with the tribal peoples in the Nilgiri Hills of South India. She had a fascinating visit with Professor Derek Freeman who believes that the Aborigines had come originally from South India, perhaps in those remote ages when the intervening seas were shallower and the chains of islands more continuous than now. In Australian museums she saw specimens of 'katta-marams' (Tamil, literally 'bound-up wood') – rafts made of logs of wood lashed together – remarkably like those used by the fishermen of India's Coromandel coast. 'Dr Freeman's photographs', Marjorie wrote in her journal, 'show people who would pass unnoticed in *many* South Indian villages and certainly in the Nilgiris/Coimbatore area'. When Marjorie visited the Ethno-Musicology Centre of the Melbourne University, she met six aborigines from Central Australia who had come to record their music there and who sang and danced for her.

In Melbourne Marjorie was shown records of Quaker families going back to ancestors who made the long voyage from Britain and pioneered the settlement of South Australia. There was much more to stimulate Marjorie's interest everywhere: the eucalyptus, in so many varieties, growing in its native land; the two Kookaburras who looked down (laughing?) from the gum tree overhead while she picnicked with friends underneath; the fascinating train journey across the South Australian desert from Melbourne at one end to Perth at the other. But it was time to leave Australia and go on.

Flight from Perth to Jakarta and Bali

After arrival in Jakarta there was just time to complete immigration and get the Garuda flight to Denpasar where she was met by her old friend, Gedong Oka. As they drove from the airport to the Oka's home in the university area, Marjorie felt she had come home already – especially that she had come to Kerala – luxuriant Kerala type vegetation, gateways, house styles with thatched roofs.

Life was suddenly much more relaxed. There was the unhurried tempo of the tropics, there were no talks to be given. On the two occasions when a talk had been arranged, it was cancelled. Gedong thought that this was because everyone was jittery about the American military situation in Southeast Asia and a 'foreign speaker' was too much of a risk. This situation gave Marjorie the opportunity to enjoy in comparative leisure the fascinating Balinese culture. She described in her journal the first of these occasions – a drive out to Ubud to the home of Gedong's friend, Mr Djokorta Agung. 'On the way we saw in the distance across the rice fields, the Balinese sacred mountain, Goenoeng Agoeng.' Mr Agung is one of an old 'princely' family and his home a typical village palace – outer court, middle court, inner court – with elaborate doorways in the walls, and a large beautiful guest house. In the village was a

118

museum with an exhibition of the work of a Balinese artist traditional in style and theme – a lovely technique of quiet gradation of sepia. Then a local performance of the gamelan orchestra and dance. 'Dusk fell as they danced, so that at the end we could not see their faces, only the slender movements – much better than trying to "improve" the situation by artificial light'.

The peaceful atmosphere of Gedong's home rested Marjorie;

I lay peacefully awake about 5 a.m. and heard Gedong's boys and girls beginning morning prayer. To my surprised pleasure someone sang the old Erse melody 'Morning hath broken' and then there were 'physical jerks' on the verandah facing the dawn.

Marjorie found herself enjoying the 'lovely early-to-bed arrangement – very natural because dawn in Bali comes gently and beautifully between 4.30 and 5 a.m. and sunset around 5 p.m.' There were a series of 'happy days with no history' where she continued 'the happy process of doing small, useful odd jobs at a leisurely pace'.

The Okas had a beach house which Gedong used periodically for two week ashram camps, and a trip there to spend several days continued the relaxed atmosphere. Marjorie walked on the beach and among the maze of quiet little lanes inland.

The high points were talks shared with Gedong about her hopes, experiences (how rich!) and plans for using this Centre. What a` wonderful couple she and her husband are; both having played a distinguished part in public (political) life, have now withdrawn to occupy themselves otherwise.

Among these 'lazy' days were two special memories – a long drive with Gedong among un-tourist-visited villages – some very old pre-Hindu villages.

We went down little grass grown side roads, we saw lovely views of mountains and sea . . . and finally walked along the paths between rice fields to a village whose headman is a relative of Gedong's. There we sat on a verandah facing a circle of hills across the fields, listening to this wise, elderly man, and eating fresh oranges. Harvesting was in full swing and every courtyard was filled with rice drying in the sun.

119

Marjorie went next to Solo to see the public health work of Mary Johnston. Mary had visited her in India during the time when she was preparing herself for this work. It was good to see the fine work she was doing, and also to be introduced to Indonesian puppets, and to the happy combination of Hindu and Muslim culture to be found there.

In Singapore I came to feel quite clearly that I should come straight home; it had not been easy to shuffle off my commitments in India for so long a period, and was only possible at all because generous friends undertook a lot of extra work; it was time to relieve them a bit. Also in spite of the *wonderful* warmth of welcome everywhere, and the joys of old friendships renewed and new ones made, I have perhaps been uprooted for long enough. So in mid-June, it felt good to get into a familiar Indian train, to see the beloved contours of the Nilgiri Hills and the friendly faces of the Kotagiri people.

CHAPTER FOURTEEN

Pendle Hill and England 1975-79

MARJORIE ARRIVED IN MADRAS that Summer of 1975, just the day after Indira Gandhi had declared a 'National Emergency'. The next year and a half was a very difficult period. Many of Marjorie's Gandhian friends were in trouble with the government, and she had a special concern for her good friend and co-worker in Nagaland, Jayaprakash Narayan, who was in prison and with very serious health problems. *The Friendly Way* had to find the right course of action in face of the 'emergency' pre-censorship rules and finally suspended publication. Printers were afraid to put out an independent paper in case it got them into trouble with the government which might confiscate their press. Marjorie herself did not feel very secure and had the feeling that her own corre-spondence was being interfered with.

Part of this period was spent at Quaker House in New Dehli, where she was able to help Arjun, the faithful Indian secretary, to prepare for the new Resident Directors whose arrival was being delayed by a variety of circumstances.

Then came an invitation to be Friend-in-Residence at Pendle Hill, a Quaker retreat and study centre near Philadelphia in the United States. She welcomed the opportunity to be part of this warm, welcoming and stimulating community as well as to have time for writing and research. In a letter to friends, Marjorie describes the writing she hoped to begin there:

> For some years now I have received periodical requests from Friends, attenders and sympathisers in India for something to read about Quaker involvement in that region. This has

made me realise that while there are a few studies of some aspects of this, and one or two biographical sketches of some of the people involved, there is nothing in any way comprehensive or up to date. In view of my own acquaintance with much of the Quaker interest in India over the last nearly 50 years, I began to wonder if I should attempt to fill the gap; and when I was able to accept an invitation to Pendle Hill, PA, during the first seven months of this year (1977), I had an opportunity of using valuable source material in USA.

There are two aspects of this Quaker history in which I am particularly interested and which I hope will find their due place in my work. One is the extent to which pieces of 'visible' Quaker service, superficially isolated, were in fact linked with one another and with Quaker thought and life elsewhere, by many 'underground' and personal threads. The other related aspect is the part played in the total picture by individual Quakers who lived in India/Pakistan/ Bangladesh in a private professional capacity. These men and women were not 'official' representatives of any Quaker body, but were nevertheless deeply concerned Friends and were often in close touch with more official Quaker activities.

I want to emphasise that I am just as interested in the impact of India upon Quakers, as of Quakers upon India. Because of this, I express my hopes to myself in thinking of this study as one of Quaker 'encounters' with India, one of a two-way traffic of ideas and influences.

Marjorie had left India in December of 1976 to spend Christmas in England with her family before going on to the United States. The year and a half between June '75 and December '76 had been filled with tension and Marjorie's health also suffered. A severe attack of malaria had her hospitalised in Madurai, where she experienced both skill and very moving kindness in a tiny private hospital run by two devoted brothers. Then, close to the time of departure for England from Bombay, flu and great weariness was followed, while she was staying with a friend in Bombay, by an acute attack of arthritis in her right hand.

What a place to choose! [wrote Marjorie]. For 24 hours I couldn't hold a pen or a spoon or comb my hair; I had to have

122

toast, etc. cut up so I could pick it up with my left hand! Well, a nice retired doctor in the flat below came and coped, with a *gentle* pain killer and alternate hot water bottles and icebags, and very soon (as you see) I could write again. I decided I would *not* postpone the flight, but British Airways provided me a young assistant at Bombay to carry things, and at London, imagine!, they produced a wheel chair!!! ME in a wheel chair! I protested that there was nothing wrong with my *legs* but they said it was the easiest routine and I submitted, for I admit I was tired by then. Dear Ellen Cumber was waiting with her little car and we were soon home here.

A relaxed period in England restored her usual good health. It had been seven years since she had seen her family and 20 years since she had spent Christmas with them and the joys of this reunion with family and friends were very healing. By the beginning of January she was off to start the winter term at Pendle Hill.

Pendle Hill

Marjorie's impact on Pendle Hill was described in the introduction Ed Sanders, Executive Clerk, gave for her public lecture there not long after she arrived:

> Unabashedly, we are referring to her already as 'Our Marjorie Sykes' as I'm sure Friends and friends do in India and in England and in Southern California, and all along that West Coast. We may not completely know who she is or what she is, but ever since the day of her arrival on this campus, we have known that she was *here*. She really is present wherever she is. Her subject this evening, 'Thou Shalt Love the Lord Thy God' is almost a keynote for the music of her daily life.

While based at Pendle Hill Marjorie was able to do considerable research for her previously described book in the Pendle Hill Library and the Friends Historical Libraries at Swarthmore and Haverford Colleges. Here visits to many India-related friends brought both the joy of reunion and inspiration for her writing. She had many invitations to visit Friends Meetings, attend conferences and give lectures in the eastern part of the United States. One of these was an Ada Howe Kent Lecture for Professor Dennis Hudson's course in Modern Indian Religious History at Smith College. Some took her as far afield as Richmond, Indiana and eastern Ohio, and to less distant places such as Washington, DC, Baltimore, and New England. She rejoiced in seeing the cherry blossoms in Washington, and at Pendle Hill 'the Spring springing in all it exciting glory. How long since I saw a real Spring?? Wonderful!'

Often in the United States – both when she travelled on the West Coast in 1975 and during this time on the East Coast – Marjorie found it hard to adjust to the personal questioning then so prevalent.

> Two young men asked me what I had gained from India 'spiritually' [she wrote]. I told them I couldn't and wouldn't answer, that any kind of verbalised answer would probably be false, over-simplified, and so superficial as to be useless – and I quoted part of Ruth Fawell's poem at them:
>
> > If you love me,
> >   please make space around me.
> > Don't do too much for me,
> >   cosset me and spoil me.
> > Don't crowd me in with probings,
> >   ask me for completely honest
> > discussion of my feelings
> >   which can sometimes be
> > so uneasy, so ill-defined
> >   that no so-called honest approach
> >   is possible.

The Henry J. Cadbury Lecture

A special opportunity was the invitation to deliver the Fifth Henry J. Cadbury Lecture which she entitled 'Freedom and the Life of the Spirit'. This is reproduced in the *Friends Journal* of 1st June, 1977. In her talk she traced the linguistic meaning of the words 'freedom', 'life', and 'spirit'. She then compared these words with Indian symbolism. She writes:

> In South India there is a town called Chidambaram. That's its Sanscrit name. Its local name is Tillai, and Tillai is said to be the centre of the universe. And in the centre of the Universe the God Shiva dances the dance of creation. The famous Indian images of the Lord of the Dance which many of you possibly have seen, emanate from this ancient South Indian tradition. Many poets have described the dance; its mystical meaning is that the centre of the universe, Tillai, is within your heart. When you realise that, you find freedom.
>
> Now this energy, this living energy, expressed in the dance – what does it mean? It means freedom manifested in disciplined order. It means freedom in balance and in harmony. Its a kind of peace, an assurance of a 'still centre,' and at one and the same time it is the adventure of spontaneous movement.

Some excerpts form her lecture show the depth of her own philosophy.

> People seem to long, with a genuine affirmation, for relationship with natural beauty, with wilderness, with soil and rock and water. But once more, this impulse is so strangely mixed with selfishness that it operates to deny these same experiences to others. Are we wiser than the simple hill tribes of South India who cannot conceive that any human being should *appropriate* any part of the earth, which to them is so clearly God's earth?

In the summer of 1977 Marjorie left the United States for what she thought would be a month or two in England before returning to India.

England

In England, however, as she pursued her research for her book on Quakers in India, she began finding 'an undreamed of wealth of information'. One thing led to another and she remained in

125

England for more than two years spending much of the time staying with Martin and Janet Ludlam in Carlisle while she did her writing. (Martin was the doctor who had cared for her in the hospital in Itarsi back in 1941. She and the Ludlams had remained friends ever since.) Her constant detective work on the book continued with one 'amazing coincidence' after another:

> I had an exciting letter this morning from a Quaker friend in Sheffield. Probings there have struck oil! The Quaker Journalist whose contribution in India I discovered has a granddaughter living – four years younger than I, married and in Somerset. She turns out to be, believe it or not, the sister-in-law of one of my close college friends!! I'm just off to the Sheffield City Library to follow up new clues she has given me.

> [20th September]: And by another amazing coincidence I tracked down and SAW the picture of the Quaker ship which made her maiden voyage to India in 1815 with dummy guns!! It was in an old farm manor house in a tiny hamlet outside Kendal now owned by a descendant of the Quaker ship owner and it is a beautiful and valuable picture.

> [16th October]: By still another amazing coincidence I have at last, just a few days ago, been able to discover *where* mercantile marine logs are kept and have written to ask permission to examine the log of the first voyage of the *Bengal*. I am hoping that there may be some entry in it which would settle once for all whether or not the 'dummy gun' story is (as the skeptics say) a fairy tale.

As these two years progressed, Marjorie was having increasing difficulty with painful arthritis in her hip. In May 1979, she wrote:

> Following Martin Ludlam's advice, I went to my brother Ronald's doctor about my hip and he referred me to a consultant whom I like very much – a frank, straight-forward Yorkshire man! We had a good talk (as much about my book and Sheffield local history as about my hip!) and his advice was to get more x-rays for him to see for himself – especially as it seemed the imbalance of my hips might be distorting my spine.

126

[10th July, 1979]: Yes, please tell any kind inquirers exactly what I've got – Osteo-arthritis, left hip only. The operation dates are confirmed: to go to hospital on 24th and get my 'spare part' on 25th. And please tell folks also that the rest of me is apparently in its usual healthy state and everyone says how *well* I look.

From Claremont Nursing Home, Sandy Gates, Sheffield:

Since becoming a 'hippo' or 'hippy' my middle name is *dormouse*; the doctor grumbles that I am practically always asleep when he drops in, and my sister, knowing me, sent a beautiful dormouse all nicely curled up for a 'get well' card. But all seems very well – I seem to be in the running for the record, having stood up on my own two feet and new hip after 2½ days and walked to the ward door. [14th August] – I was discharged on 10th August, the 17th day after the operation . . . and brought back to Ronald's home.

Marjorie was lovingly cared for during all this period by her brother, Ronald, and his wife, Mary, until by December 1979 she was ready to head back to India. She wrote in a general letter to friends:

I never dreamed that the projected book about *Quakers in India* would take me more than two years. It turned into a kind of detective enterprise – discovering people whose contributions in India have either been forgotten or never known. There are probably other 'unknowns', but for better or worse I have at last brought it to an end; once publication matters are settled I shall go and book that flight.

Her book, *Quakers in India*, published by George Allen and Unwin, came out on 30th October, 1980.

CHAPTER FIFTEEN

Rasulia 1979-88

BEFORE SHE LEFT ENGLAND, Marjorie had accepted an invitation to make her future base at Rasulia, where she had spent time so often over the years helping out when there was need. The invitation had come from the Governing Board and the new Coordinator, Partap Aggarwal, whom Marjorie had known as a young 'volunteer' 30 years before. Partap was very keen that Rasulia should experiment seriously with 'natural farming', abandoning the use of chemical fertilisers and pesticides, and trying to demonstrate healthy and successful practices for the sake of the village farmers around. This was something very close to Marjorie's own heart, and she was happy to be part of the community.

She describes her new responsibilities thus:

> Personally I find lots to do. I help where I can informally, and this usually includes seeing that guests are comfortable as well as a variety of jobs such as looking after the library, being treasurer, also being a general 'grannie'. We sometimes enjoy some really 'pukka' coffee from Madras. I'm not the only one who enjoys good Madras coffee and various people know when a morning 'cuppa' is likely to be available in my kitchen, and drop in. I have one room in the guest house which is just an ordinary family house; there are two other 'double' guest rooms and a little dining room and kitchen, and there is an alternation of company and solitude which is very acceptable.

Friends who visited there describe her care of guests:

> She ran that guest house, mending mosquito nets, doing the cooking with a kerosene camp burner, unless the methane

128

generator was working, scavenged fruit from the jungle and cooked coarse grains, and served a constant stream of young foreigners who came to see what was going on. She herself had a simple white-washed room where all of her working needs were efficiently arranged, and from which she did her writing and correspondence; she daily washed by hand her worn Kurta-pajamas. She fussed at the guests if they were not disciplined and sat at the table chatting, so she couldn't get on with her work (or even sometimes if they didn't arrange the chairs at the table the way she would have done) and wouldn't let anyone help with the washing up. Her habits of disciplined life in the ashram and in her own work were strong and lifelong.

Although the main thrust of the work at Rasulia is towards showing how a village may become self-reliant in the provision of its basic needs of food, clothing and shelter, different administrators had different approaches and the transition from one to another was not always easy. Friends of many years remember:

Marjorie had had the experience of being on the Board of Friends Rural Centre in Rasulia for many years, and, as we have seen it evolve for 40 years, we know what an undertaking that has been. Each group of Friends brought a very different focus. With each change – and we were at Rasulia during one of them – workers had to change. Through it all Marjorie, as I understand it, recruited new directors, filled in herself between times, and was a liaison with British Friends and their financing. Marjorie kept Rasulia going between directors, but was also a strong enough person in her own ideas that it must have been a little hard for the directors sometimes.

In a letter to a friend in March 1981 Marjorie describes the main emphasis during that time:

The air is thick with experiments in 'energy'. Gobar gas plant, very successful, and lots of experiments in manufacturing efficient burners out of mud and old tiles so that they come within the practical possibilities of a villager. Also solar cookers. We imported *one* from Gujarat and are similarly engaged in trying for a cheap home-made one. It happily cooks a whole series of things – rice, dal, vegetables, etc., bread and cake, also baked potatoes and sweet potatoes and makes excellent kheer. All in about two hours – but if you leave it in, it won't burn. Of course, the sun must shine, so one must have an alternative when it doesn't; and it won't do chappatis or puris, of course.

Marjorie helped with the organising of Quaker Conferences at Rasulia during the 80's; they were usually held in February, when the weather was neither too cold nor too hot and farming demands were not heavy. The one in 1983 had 25 participants not counting those living at Rasulia. Their discussion centred around a question troubling many of them. 'Can you be a Quaker without becoming a Christian?' And concluded that it is enough to recognise one another as Quakers and not to use divisive labels or distinctions whether of religious or national background.

One of the participants was Paulina Titus, a senior Friend who had recently been widowed, and who lived with one of her sons and his wife in their family home not far away. Her son, Raju, was deeply interested in natural farming and had set to work to practice it in his spare time on their few acres of by no means first class land. In the meeting Paulina insisted that what counts is to experience the transforming power which comes from within; Marjorie suggested that we need the strength of both wings, 'Christ centred' and 'Universalist', in order to fly.

In February 1984, 40 people came, sharing their work and their visions for the future. The group assembled under the large, spreading banyan tree for worship and under the peepal tree for discussion. The spiritual depth that permeated everything made the whole gathering a real religious experience. Marjorie, as recording clerk, wrote that there was

> a creative tension between the concern that we should develop the habit of thinking globally and the conviction that what counts is living what we believe.

Banwari Lal Chaudhri has expressed his appreciation of being able to learn the Quaker-way of life from Marjorie, and still be encouraged to keep his Hindu Culture intact.

Letters to friends reveal some of the more informal, day to day joys of Marjorie's life:

We found some months ago a 10 foot snake-skin out of which its owner had walked, head first, leaving it in *perfect* condition. (Harmless, beneficent snake.) As it remained undeteriorated I sent it by an English visiting Friend to my brother who *loves* such things. Yes, Ronald and Mary are thrilled with the snake-skin; Mary describes it draped over the grandfather clock, as she says, a bit of natural beauty and a bit of man-made beauty together.

[6th February, 1982]: Imagine me writing with a lovely golden cat sitting on my lap, keeping me warm (It's still unusually cold). Did I ever tell you about Oliver? He turned up one evening while I was eating supper, a dirty, frightened, starving adolescent kitten. I couldn't bear it and fed him, and slowly he lost his fear of humanity, beginning with me, and after a few days began to purr and then to wash himself revealing a beautiful leopard-marked golden coat. He is Oliver because like Oliver Twist in the story, he 'asks for more'. Like Oliver, he doesn't always get it, but he's now a healthy muscular cat,

Peepul Tree

131

and since the day he took up residence, rats and mice have ceased to trouble the house!

Along with Marjorie's continuing responsibilities at Rasulia, she was working, along with Jehangir Patel, on a book of personal memories of Gandhi. Marjorie and Jehangir had been friends since they first met in Gandhi's Ashram in 1944. Both had entered Cambridge University at the same time in 1923, but didn't know each other then. Jehangir, a business man in Bombay, and Marjorie were in the process of combining their memories into a book, *Gandhi: His Gift of the Fight* which was published by Rasulia in April 1987.

There had been short trips to England during these Rasulia years too. A short two month visit June–August 1984 to see family and friends, and again in 1986 to research material for a history of the Friends Rural Centre at Rasulia which was approaching its centenary year. She found a lot of revealing personal correspondence – some in Friends House, the Central offices and library for British Friends in London, and more in old family letters found up and down the country.

Banyan Tree

Back at Rasulia, Marjorie received word of the death of her brother, Ronald, on 15th April, 1987. She wrote:

> I say 'sad' news but I'm not at all sure that is the right word. Life has been such a struggle for Ronald for months now, with constant pain and increasing difficulty in moving about at all, and anxiety about his wife, Mary, who became more and more seriously confused. . . . *Dear* Ronald, he was such a *kind*, compassionate person as well as an upright one, and it's all those things that I want to remember about him now. . . . One has to remember that the Self is something deeper and more abiding than either body or 'mind'.

In July of 1987 Marjorie received an invitation to be 'Chief Guest' at the closing ceremony of the celebration of Tagore's 125th Anniversary in Bombay, 10th August. She had also been asked to give the 'Presidential Address' to the Friends Historical Society, UK, for 1987 which meant returning to England in the Autumn. In August, Marjorie went to Bombay for the Tagore celebration and then on to New Delhi on 14th September to collect her visa for UK.

In October she was back in England to give the 'Presidential Address', entitled *Unfinished Pilgrimages: Geoffrey Maw and Jack Hoyland in India*. Both men were British Quakers who had begun their work in India during the years preceding the first world war. Geoffrey Maw was probably the *only* non-Indian to make the great pilgrimage to the source of the Ganges *as a pilgrim*, in the days when one walked the whole way from Rishikesh.

Jack Hoyland's pilgrimage was a pilgrimage in thought, especially in educational thought, a search for 'wholeness' of physical well-being, mental alertness and spiritual understanding _ the same concern that Gandhi was to place before India 20 years later. This lecture was published in the *Journal of the Friends Historical Society*, Volume 35 No. 7, 1989.

The two men, contemporaries and close personal friends, each had a deep respect for the other's pilgrim path. They shared a longing to understand and learn from India's saints and thinkers; they shared an understanding of Quakerism not as a mere sect, but as a witness to the vitalising force of the Spirit.

133

The job done, Marjorie returned to India and was in time to share in the happy occasion at the beginning of 1988 when Masanobu Fuknoka, the Japanese scientist-farmer whose work had inspired Rasulia's natural farming, himself paid a personal visit. He was pleased with Rasulia, and even more pleased with Raju's farm. Immediately afterwards Partap and his family left, because the atmospheric pollution caused by the large Government paper mill which had been built on the westward, windward side of Rasulia resulted in such serious health problems for his wife. Marjorie stayed on, doing what she could to help the community and the new coordinator, until the autumn, when she accepted an invitation to be a Friend in Residence at Woodbrooke College.

CHAPTER SIXTEEN

England – Woodbrooke – Swarthmore 1988-93

THE WOODBROOKE INVITATION enabled Marjorie to embark on a new piece of research and writing. She describes her project in a letter to 'friends everywhere':

> For some time there has been an idea abroad that something ought to be written about the history of the Friends Rural Centre at Rasulia in its Quaker context – especially as the Centre is close to its Centenary. . . . But Rasulia's Quaker context, for nearly 60 years, has been much wider than the Hoshangabad district in which it is situated, and its doings cannot be fully understood apart from the other aspects of Quaker work in the Sub-continent both before and after Independence. So it is a big undertaking and I feel sure it is worth trying to do it well.

The research which followed revealed the fact that the story told in *Quakers in India* was in some ways one-sided and incomplete. The book itself was by then out of print, and it seemed appropriate that the Rasulia 'Centenary' project should take the form of a new and more comprehensive account of Friends' encounters with India. The proposed title is *A Human Tapestry*, to indicate how closely Friendly enterprises have been and are interwoven with those of others in a fabric of goodwill and high endeavour.

In August 1989, Marjorie attended London Yearly Meeting's residential session in Aberdeen, Scotland. She was often seen sewing and a sketch of her so engaged was done by the Quaker artist, Margaret Glover, and has since been printed on a post card, now familiar to many Friends. This led to future sessions with Margaret, one of which is described in a letter to P. T. Thomas in India, dated 8th September, 1989:

> You'll never guess how this letter is being written. I'm sitting at a table in Clapham, quite near to the place where William Wilberforce and all his Quaker friends planned their campaign against the slave trade, having my portrait painted!!! One of the Quaker trusts has commissioned a Quaker woman artist to do a series of 'peace workers' for the Bradford University Peace Department and I have been dragged in!!! A new experience for me – I'm staying with the artist, Margaret Glover, in her Clapham flat. During the first sitting I sat in a sort of dentist chair doing nothing; that didn't work out well and was scrapped; this second one seems to be coming out better. I did the accompanying *Friendly Way* list during yesterday's sitting, and now I'm writing letters.

Sketch of Marjorie by Margaret Glover at London Yearly Meeting in Aberdeen 1989

In December 1989, Marjorie visited India again; there was work to be done at Rasulia, material to be collected for the book and old friends to visit. She went first to Rasulia, and then for a Christmas visit to Victoria Armstrong in Kotagiri as the first stage of a planned tour in the South.

Then things went wrong. Tired after the long journey from Hoshangabad, she spent a good deal of time in bed during the next few days. However, she found it difficult to sleep due to a persistent cough. She wanted to consult Ramamurthy (Ram), Asia Secretary for Quaker Peace and Service, and her good friend, who happened to be in India then visiting his family in Madras. She wrote to him in care of his sister in Madras and also phoned his brother, Sunder, in Bombay to be sure where he was.

Meanwhile, Victoria Armstrong became alarmed at Marjorie's condition and herself telephoned Sunder, hoping he could reach Ram to ask him to come at once. Sunder reached Ram who took the first available berth on the train and arrived in Kotagiri the next morning. They all agreed that Marjorie should return to Madras with Ram where there were better medical facilities. The next day Ram and Marjorie were off in a taxi to Mettupalaiyam and the train. Although they had no reservations, they fortunately got two berths on the night train. Ram, worried about Marjorie's condition, stayed awake throughout the long night journey in case of need. Looking back, one realises that his quick action and devoted care probably saved her life.

In Madras she was taken to her old 'home' in the Bentinck School – St Christopher's College compound and was welcomed to stay. Still being unwell, she was helped by Sorojini Balreddy, her friend and Principal of the College, to contact her doctor friend who advised her to go to the Rainy Hospital where she had once sent so many student nurses for training. To her great astonishment she was then taken off to the Intensive Care Unit. The first two days she was gravely ill and the consultant doctor asked Ram to inform her next of kin and he phoned her sister, Kathleen, in England. As the doctor later explained to Marjorie, her various troubles were all due to 'cardiac valve failure' – that the old pump was wearing out and would in the future need assistance to do its job.

As a great believer in fresh air and simple treatments, being in the air-conditioned hospital with various support systems did not appeal to her, knowing that outside was the lovely January sun and delicious sea breeze. What she really wanted was a hot-water bottle. However, she remembers with thankfulness the skill and loving care of a very fine hospital.

After two days her condition improved enough that she was able to have four visitors at once: Ram and his wife Stephanie, P. T. Thomas from Bangalore and another old friend, Krishnammal from Madurai.

After nine days in the hospital, she went back to St Christopher's College for a month's rest. In early March she was allowed to fly to Bombay. Then, accompanied by Ram, she flew to England and was able to return to Woodbroke and her writing. When in accordance with instructions she visited the cardiologist in Birmingham,

Portrait of Marjorie by Margaret Glover

138

The Garden at Swarthmore

she swelled with pride at his praise for the thoroughness of the Rainy Hospital report.

Later that month Marjorie wrote to a friend:

> One friend in UK wrote a day or two ago that she had felt me so close that she thought I might have died – but it turned out that I was merely writing to her!! According to what I *now* hear, I *might* have died in Madras, though I didn't feel particularly ill and was quite capable of arguing with the *dear* nurses about features of the Intensive Care Unit of which I didn't approve! I really am feeling fitter and fitter.

Then, at Woodbrooke, on 10th May, the day before her 85th birthday, the old nagging cough began again. This time she recognised the symptoms and called for help. The ambulance arrived almost immediately and so did Margaret Gray from her home on the campus. The emergency care received right there in the ambulance and en route to the hospital relieved her symptoms and she could be admitted at once without going into the Emergency section. Margaret stayed on into the night with her until she was completely settled and was a great comfort. By the next morning all was well and a birthday cake was brought from Woodbrooke and shared with the nurses and other patients in the ward. She was kept a few days more under observation. It was decided that the medication prescribed in Madras, though a regular treatment for her condition, did not suit her, and a satisfactory alternative was found.

True to form, Marjorie was writing letters the following day – 12th May – and wrote to a friend:

> One bonus is that as I sat gasping in that chair on Thursday night and wondering if I were really going to pass out there and then, I found myself perfectly content to accept whatever came. All the same I'm glad in many ways to be still alive in this truly wonderful world, and hope in a few weeks to enjoy English wild roses once more.

Happily she did.

Over the years Marjorie had become a much loved member of Woodbrooke's international community. She took part in the daily Quaker meetings for worship, sometimes giving a clear powerful message that came from a life-time of waiting on the Spirit. She

Marjorie and Martha Dart at Swarthmore

140

worked in the library, in her room, and often liked to sit reading or talking to a friend in an upstairs sitting room with a beautiful view over the grounds in front of her.

During that summer term in 1990, Marjorie made an exciting discovery in a box of Geoffrey Maw's papers in the Selly Oak Colleges' central library. She found a file full of material about the Narmada River, the life of the human populations who depend on it, its rapids and waterfalls, sacred sites and pilgrimages. The notes were 50 years old and often brittle with age, and with the encouragement of Hugh and Daphne Maw, she worked on editing and publishing them. She worked hard on them that summer vacation in London, and sent them to friends in India for printing. There were delays, but the little book was ready by the Spring of 1992 – *Narmada, The Life of a River*.

Christmas 1991 was spent with Benjamin and Emily Polk, old friends from India, in a village near Salisbury. On Christmas Day itself, Marjorie came down with Shingles, and although it was treated immediately and effectively, it sapped her energy for a number of months. She decided to look for a place where she could settle down undisturbed to concentrate on her writing.

She knew of one Quaker retirement community, 'Swarthmore' in Gerrards Cross, in the Chiltern Hills, pleasant country and only a half-hour by train from Central London. They were able to take her as a 'long-term' guest from January 1991. There was

> a good garden full of birds and lovely trees, friendly folk and a doctor who comes once a week – a personal friend of the one who cared for me so well in Salisbury.

She soon found that in addition to all this, the house had Indian connections. The Friends had bought it about 1945. Before that it had been the home of an Irish family and was called Cooldara. At least one of the family worked in India and had connections with Friends there; another had been a great friend of Muriel Lester, who was Gandhi's hostess when he visited England for the Round Table Conference in 1931, and Gandhi had spent one of his weekends at Cooldara. Public records of that time do not mention it (it was of no political importance) but old residents of Gerrards Cross, now living in 'Swarthmore', have clear memories of his coming.

141

Marjorie in her room at Swarthmore

Marjorie had previously received word from the Visva-Bharati University at Santiniketan that she had been proposed to receive their highest academic honour, the Desikottama (Doctor of Literature). When the date for the convocation was set for 21st March, 1992, she was unable to attend. The citation was presented by the Upacharya (Vice Chancellor) and the award was conferred by the Acharya (Chancellor) *in absentia*. The citation given on that day follows:

> The Upacharya presents the name of Srimati Marjorie Sykes to the Acharya and requests him to confer on Srimati Marjorie Sykes the Honorary Degree of Desikottama (Doctor of Literature) *in absentia*.

RESPECTED ACHARYA

On the occasion of this Convocation Anniversary I beg to present the name of Srimati Marjorie Sykes, a great lover of peace, a zealous educator and a writer of repute, as one richly deserving the highest honour that this University can confer.

Hailing from a simple Yorkshire family and brought up in a village of miners, she assimilated from her father, a school teacher, the spirit of service and a reverence for life. As a student at Cambridge, she learnt to accept the precepts of the Bible, especially the ideal of non-violence. Her desire to serve brought her to India as a young woman, and she taught at various places in India. The Quaker faith helped her to combine the noble traditions of our country and the spiritual ideals of her native faith into a living unity. Soon she was inspired by Mahatma Gandhi and followed his ideals of *ahimsa* and *satya*. Invited by Rabindranath, she joined the ashram at Santiniketan in 1939 as a teacher of English. Like her famous compatriot, C. F. Andrews, whose first biography she wrote, she served as a living link between these two great personalities, Mahatma Gandhi and Gurudeva Rabindranath, striving to learn from them both equally and impart their insights to others. Srimati Marjorie Sykes learnt Bengali and translated a number of Rabindranath's writings into her mother-tongue, she also wrote a simple and moving biography of Rabindranath for her students.

When Marjorie Sykes left Santinketan in 1947, she joined Mahatma Gandhi at Sevagram. She has written inspiringly of the life in Santiniketan and among Gandhians, it is a testimony of her deep sincerity in the search for truth and of her committed love for our country of which she became a citizen after Independence. More recently she has spent many years experimenting with biological farming in Madhya Pradesh expressing thus her concern for ecological balance in our country.

Travelling untiringly in India and abroad, Marjorie Sykes spread the message of peace, setting an example by her own modest and simple life-style and her unassailable optimism. She embodies what is best in our culture and in her native European tradition. Through-out her life, she has been committed to the ideals held dear by Rabindranath, spreading them beyond the bounds of India. Summing up her life in a single sentence, we may say that she has above all been, in the best Quaker tradition, a true friend of friends.

In accordance with the desire expressed by the teachers and workers of Visva-Bharati assembled here on the occasion of this Convocation Anniversary, I submit that in recognition of Srimati Marjorie Sykes' unflinching search for truth and her deep and committed love for India and Rabindranath, you may be pleased to confer on her, in accordance with the Statutes of Visva-Bharati, the highest honour of this University.

The Acharya confers the Degree on Srimati Marjorie Sykes.

UPACHARYA,

In recognition of her great qualities and achievements, I, as the Acharya of Visva- Bharati, confer on Srimati Marjorie Sykes the Degree of Desikottama (Doctor of Literature) *in absentia* and request you to convey the same to her.

Very soon after Marjorie's arrival at 'Swarthmore' she got another 'supplementary' job to do. Some years earlier, while she was still at Rasulia, she had been asked to make an English translation of a book of excerpts from Vinoba Bhave's writings which his fellow workers had put together after his death in 1982. In the course of his many speeches he had used incidents from his own life to illustrate his point, and these have been arranged as *Glimpses of a Life Story*. At Rasulia Marjorie had been too busy to undertake this, but in 1991 the request was renewed. She had already in earlier years made a number of translations from Vinoba, especially his *Thoughts on Education*, and was eager that his crisp, down-to-earth Hindi should be reflected in the English. She agreed, and during the following two years this was done in the intervals of the 'major' work *Human Tapestry*. As she says when there is danger of getting stale, there is something else to do instead.

Following on the *Narmada* book, Marjorie found another 'supplementary' piece of work, to edit in collaboration with Geoffrey Maw's daughter, Gillian Conacher, the journals and papers in which Geoffrey recorded his Himalayan pilgrimages, and which are of very great interest, although they have so far remained unpublished.

And there we may leave her, in her comfortable chair by her 'basement' window at 'Swarthmore' with a 'grassroots' view of the sloping lawn outside and the birds in the bushes whenever she looks up from the clipboard and the current writing on her knee.

The Life of the Spirit

'IN THE QUIET ROOM at Woodbrooke Marjorie was with us in Meeting for Worship – a gaunt, frail figure who emanated a remarkable depth of stillness and strength. She stood up and without hesitation recited Isaiah 6, verses 1-8 in all the richness of the King James Version.

1 *In the year that King Uzziah died, I saw the Lord sitting upon a throne, high and lifted up, and his train filled the temple.*

2 *Above him stood the Seraphim: each one had six wings; with twain he covered his face, with twain he covered his feet, and with twain he did fly.*

3 *And one cried to another, and said 'Holy, holy, holy, is the Lord of hosts: the whole earth is filled with His glory'.*

4 *And the foundations of the thresholds were moved at the voice of him that cried, and the house was filled with smoke.*

5 *Then said I, 'Woe is me! for I am undone; because I am a man of unclean lips, and I dwell in the midst of a people of unclean lips; for mine eyes have seen the King, the Lord of hosts'.*

6 *Then flew one of the Seraphim unto me, having a live coal in his hands, which he had taken with tongs from off the altar:*

7 *And he touched my mouth with it, and said, 'Lo, this hath touched thy lips; and thine iniquity is taken away, and thy sin purged'.*

8 *And I heard the voice of the Lord, saying, 'Whom shall I send, and who will go for us?' Then I said, 'Here am I: send me'.*

'She, who had answered God's "Whom shall I send?" so often in her life, was standing there undaunted, ready (in her late 70's) . . . "Here am I, send me".

'It was as if the vivid experience of the writer of Isaiah and the reality of this woman were as one in those words.'

Sources Used

PROLOGUE
   a. Maggie (Margaret) Stein Squire
   b. Margaret Moore
   c. Martha Dart in *Friends Journal,* January 1, 1973

Gandhi: His Gift of the Fight, J. Patel and M. Sykes, Friends Rural Centre, Rasulia, 1987

'Roots and Fruits', *The Visvabharati Quarterly* New Series Vol. 1 Nos. 3-4, 1991

Marjorie's own autobiographical sketches

Marjorie on tape and in personal conversations

'Memories 1939-41', *The Visvabharati Quarterly* New Series, Vol. 2, Nos. 1-4, 1991

Visva-Bharati – An Indian Poet's University, Friends Service Council

Rabindranath Tagore, by M. Sykes, Orient Longman, 1943

The Wayfarer

Marjorie's Journal Letters to Friends Service Council – Friends House Library

Minutes of India Committee – Friends House Library

The Task of Peacemaking: Reports of the World Pacifist Meeting, Santiniketan and Sevagram, 1949

Personal letters

Memories of Friends

The Friendly Way

The Friendly Woman

The Australian Friend

New Zealand Friends Newsletter

Friends Bulletin

Marjorie's Travel Journal around Pacific Rim

The Friend

Friends Journal

Journal of the Friends Historical Society, Vol. 35, No. 35, 1989

'C. F. Andrews: The Unfinished Revolution', Andrews Memorial Lecture at St Stephen's College – February 12, 1972

Log Books at Woodbrooke College

'Staying on at Home: 1928-88', *Indo-British Review: A Journal of History*, 1988

'Friends and World Religions', from Study Booklet – *Sharing our Faith*, FWCC, 1959

'What All Religions Have in Common', from *Journal of the Blaisdell Institute*, Vol. XI, No. 1, Spring-Summer 1976)

'Friends and Young India', Horace G. Alexander in Friends Service Council pamphlet

Foundations of Living, M. Sykes, Parisar 1988, 'Yamuna' ICS Colony, Ganeshkhind Rd., Pune 411 007

The Earth is the Lord's: Shri Vinoba Bhave and the Land, M. Sykes, Friends Peace Committee, Friends House

EPILOGUE
Jenifer Faulkner

Glossary of Indian Words

Ahimsa	respect for all living things and avoidance of violence towards others both in thought and deed
amma	mother
Aryan	a member of the peoples speaking any of the languages of the Indo-European family
ashram	the abode of a guru and disciples
Bengali	relating to the province of Bengal or its people or language
Brahmin	a person of the highest Hindu caste
chappati	flat unleavened bread, made of wholemeal flour
dhoti	waist cloth worn by a man
Dravidian	relating to the original people of South India and Sri Lanka
guru	an influential teacher, a revered mentor
khadi	handspun and handwoven cotton cloth
kurta	a loose shirt or tunic
maidan	an open space in or near a town
mandapam	an open hall, with a flat roof supported on columns
mandir	temple
pukka	genuine, of good quality
Qur'an	the Islamic sacred book
Sarvodaya	the welfare of all, the new social order advocated by Gandhi (sarva = all, udaya = rising)
satya	truth, reality
Srimati	Miss, a title of respect
Tamil	a language of the Dravidian peoples of South India and Sri Lanka
Upanishad	sacred texts, regarded as the completion of the Vedas
Vedas	the most ancient Hindu scriptures

Marjorie Sykes' Published Writings

BOOKS

Rabindranath Tagore
Longmans, Green & Co. Ltd., 1943

Charles Freer Andrews
Marjorie Sykes with Benarsidas Chaturvedi
George Allen and Unwin Ltd. London, 1949
Reprinted in India, October 1971 (Asvina, 1983)
Published by the Director, Publications Division,
Ministry of Information and Broadcasting,
Government of India, Patiala House, New Delhi

Education in Search of a Philosophy
Indian Council of Basic Education,
Gandhi Shikshan Bhavan, Juhu, Bombay 400 054, 1976

Quakers in India: A Forgotten Century
George Allen and Unwin, 1980

Gandhi: His Gift of the Fight
by Jehangir P. Patel and Marjorie Sykes
Friends Rural Centre, 1987
Rasulia, Hoshangabad, M.P. 461 001

PAMPHLETS and ESSAYS

Gandhiji, A special volume of essays
Chapter 'The Influence of Christian Thought on Ghandhiji'
Compiled to be given to Gandhi on his 75th birthday in 1944
Copy in Friends House Library, London

Love, Law, and War (The politics of Jesus)
Pamphlet for the Fellowship of Reconciliation in India
The Earth is the Lord's
Shri Vinoba Bhave and the Land
Friends Peace Committee,
Friends House, Euston Road, London NWI
What Are the Quakers?
The Quaker Centre, Delhi, 1955
'Friends and World Religions'
Study Booklet – *Sharing Our Faith,* FWCC, 1959
Foundations of Living
Parisar, 1988
'Yamuna', I.C.S. Colony Ganeshkhind Road, Pune 411 007

ARTICLES in MAGAZINES

'Membership in the Society of Friends'
The Friends Quarterly, Vol. 9, 1955, pp. 172-176
'Community Through Work and Prayer'
The Friends Quarterly, Vol. 11, 1957, pp. 61-69
'Buy Daffodils'
The Friend, March 13, 1970
'The Breaking of Bread'
The Friend, April 16, 1971
'"Deenabandhu" Andrews – Rebel and Saint'
Indian and Foreign Review, December, 1971
'The Essential Unity of Living Religions'
Friends Journal, January 1, 1974
'The Spiritual Basis of Simplicity'
Friends Journal, May 1, 1976
'Reflections on a Journey'
Friends World News – Northern Hemisphere, Autumn 1976
                    Southern Hemishphere, Spring 1976
'Breaking Down the Walls'
The Friend, February 25, 1977

'Staying on, at Home: 1928-88'
Indo-British Review: A Journal of History, 1988
'Roots and Fruits'
Visvabharati Quarterly, New Series, Vol. I, Nos. 3-4, 1991-92
'Memories 1939-41'
Visvabharati Quarterly, New Series, Vol. 2, Nos. 1-4, 1991
'Memories and Reflections', Church of South India inaugurated 1947, Church of North India, 1970
Pilgrim, the magazine of the Friends of the Church of India, March, 1993

LECTURES

'C. F. Andrews: The Unfinished Revolution'
The Andrews Memorial Lecture – St Stephen's College
February 12, 1972
'What All Religions Have in Common'
Journal of the Blaisdell Institute, Vol. XI, No. 1, Spring 1976
'Freedom and the Life of the Spirit'
5th Henry J. Cadbury Lecture
Friends Journal, June 1, 1977
'Unfinished Pilgrimages: Geoffrey Maw and Jack Hoyland in India'
Presidential Lecture for the Friends Historical Society given 17 October, 1987
Journal of the Friends Historical Society, Vol. 55, No. 7, 1989

EDITED

C. F. Andrews: Representative Writings
Compiled and Edited by Marjorie Sykes, April, 1973
National Book Trust, New Delhi, India

Narmada: The Life of a River
by Geoffrey Waring Maw. Edited and published by Marjorie Sykes
Distributed by Friends Rural Centre, 1922
Rasulia, Hoshangabad, M.P. 461 001

TRANSLATIONS

Thoughts on Education, by Vinoba Bhave
Translated by Marjorie Sykes

Index

Map of India showing Marjorie Sykes' main points of interest